About the

Francesca Amber Sawyer is originally from Canvey Island, Essex. She now resides in Camden, inner London. In the period between moving from Essex to London, she became personally involved with a Premiership footballer and was featured in tabloid newspapers such as *The Sun*. This and subsequent experiences form the basis of her first book, *WAG Don't-Wannabe*. Francesca also writes for several fashion magazines and websites. She is currently planning her second book, on London life and dating. Find out more at www.francescaamber.com

WAG
Don't-
Wannabe

WAG Don't-Wannabe

The Smart Girl's Guide to Footballers

Francesca Amber Sawyer

First published in paperback 2008
by Pennant Books

Text copyright © 2008 Francesca Amber Sawyer

The moral right of the author has been asserted.

British Library Cataloguing-in-Publication Data:
A catalogue record for this book is available on request from
The British Library

ISBN 978-1-906015-30-5

Design & Typeset by Envy Design Ltd

Printed in the UK by CPI William Clowes Beccles NR34 7TL

Front cover illustration © Andy Wadsworth Design.
Back cover photo copyright © Kev Rush/Planet Photos.

Pennant Books
A division of Pennant Publishing Ltd
PO Box 5675
London W1A 3FB

www.pennantbooks.com

ACKNOWLEDGEMENTS

If you look up 'How to write acknowledgements' on Wiki Answers, you get a simple instruction: "Type 'thank you'." Helpful as this may be, it doesn't cover everything I want to say to the people who have been instrumental in helping me to write this book.

My immense gratitude goes to Richard, my agent, who first believed that there was a story to be told, and also to Cass, Paul and Philomena at Pennant Books for giving me this opportunity. Thanks to Chris at *The People*, for taking a chance on making me into front-page news and perceiving a much bigger story than the naming and shaming of yet another cheating footballer.

Speaking of which, thank you to 'Wesley' and all of the footballers I've been fortunate/unfortunate enough to meet. Your actions, both good and bad, have inspired *WAG Don't-Wannabe* in more ways than you'll ever know. I hope that you're not angry, but that you see that we all have our own goals in life – and our own ways of achieving them.

Thank you, Mum – you do so much for me and I'll never know why. I hope that this book will somehow make you proud. (Can you please stop telling everyone you meet about it now?) Thanks also to my dad and my grandparents, for teaching me to love reading and always encouraging me to write. I'm so sorry this book isn't about ponies!

Thank you to all my friends. You really are 'the family that you choose'. To Jennifer, Nicola Kimble, Claire and Joanne, among many others – your support means more than I ever thought to tell you. Thanks Holly, Kayla and Laura, who have helped me to settle into my new London life, for sharing their love of this wonderful city we call home. Without you, lots of 'research' for this book would not have been possible. It's been the most fun – but, as we've feared all along, now it's over we'll have to find other excuses for our appalling behaviour!

Finally, this book is dedicated to the one person who has listened to my plans, day and night, for the last year. She has been my shoulder to cry on at my lowest point, and will be the first person I celebrate with when the first copy of this book is sold. I couldn't have done it without you, my dear sister.

We can talk about something else now, I promise …

For Anouska

CONTENTS

TIMELINE OF EVENTS

February 2006

I meet 'the Footballer' in Newcastle on my 21st birthday.

Begin writing *Essex Girl in London* blog.

May 2007

I meet Wesley, this book's central male figure, in a club in Kensington. We begin what will become a seven-month relationship.

June 2007

I discover that Wesley isn't really 'Wesley' at all – but a footballer with a long-term girlfriend and a child. Despite feelings of guilt, I am unable to end the relationship.

November 2007

A major tabloid newspaper is informed about our relationship by a friend. I am interrogated by Wesley and his lawyers. The story is dropped thanks to a legal document they urge me to sign.

December 2007

I attend the Christmas party held by Wesley's football club. The seedy world of Premiership footballers becomes ever clearer to me ... I decide I need to end the relationship.

I give an interview for a story which does not name Wesley, but reveals what goes on behind the façade of Premiership football, with *The People*.

February 2008

Sparked off by a nasty story about me in *The Sun*, I find myself sitting on the sofa with *Richard and Judy*, explaining about a book I'm writing. As of this point, I haven't yet written a word.

March 2008

Pennant Books offer me a deal, and *WAG Don't-Wannabe – The Smart Girl's Guide to Footballers* is born. Besides recounting my own experiences, I recognise that it has to reach the widest possible market – so I advise girls on how to go about meeting footballers too. Despite my negative experiences, I still understand their aspirations.

October 2008

WAG Don't-Wannabe is finished, and footballers are banished to the 'past' section of my love life – forever!

WHO'S WHO? – YOUR GUIDE TO PSEUDONYMOUS FIGURES IN THIS BOOK

"When I am dead, I hope it is said, [her] sins were scarlet but [her] books were read."
– (with apologies to) Hilaire Belloc

"So what if I sexualise things? I'll sexualise you in a minute." – Russell Brand

A little something before you begin reading …

Although I'm spilling the beans on my life and those around me, I'm not so callous as to land those involved in the shit, a la Karrine Steffans.* They know who they are and that's enough for me. I've changed their names – because I'm nice like that – so if you ever find yourself getting confused between a rendezvous with Wesley and an ill-fated trip to St Tropez with Club Boy, then check out my key:

*AKA Superhead, *author of Confessions of a* Video Vixen – *it's a great book, read it!*

WESLEY: The most prominent figure in this book and the reason I'm writing it. He's a Premiership football player who plays for England and lives in London. We had a seven-month affair and he totally broke my heart. I'm not supposed to admit it, as I'm meant to be super-independent and over him, but I would take him back in a second for just one more hot night! I started seeing him whilst I had a boyfriend, which I'm not proud of. Worse still, we first met in the club that my boyfriend of the time owned. (Not cool.) He fooled me into a relationship with him by pretending to be a personal trainer and all-round regular nice guy.

FOOTBALLER: My first pro football dalliance, whom I met on my 21st birthday. He plays for a big Premiership team up north, and has the most amazing talent. (You would have to see it to believe it! Can you guess … ?) We casually saw each other, albeit only rarely, for over a year.

CLUB BOY: My ex-boyfriend, who owns one of London's hottest clubs. I ended up dating him out of boredom, as I was practically living in the Hilton hotel, Park Lane, at the time. (Can you believe they only have twelve in-room movies, and half of those are shit? I'd seen them all twice.) He asked me out to dinner and a club opening party, and who would refuse him? He's one of the sweetest guys I know, and will make someone a perfect (if slightly hairy and sweaty) husband one day.

FRANKIE: One of the biggest international soccer players to

come out of America. I visited him on the continent for one weekend only.

PIERRE: French Premiership footballer I briefly got involved with, strictly as research for this book. (That's my story and I'm sticking to it!)

FOREWORD

"For me, there are three things in life I don't tolerate and those are liars, cheats and thieves. Unfortunately, what I've been led to believe about many football players is that they normally fit into one or more of those categories."
– former WAG Cassie Sumner

If you're expecting this book to tell you how to catch the man of your dreams, a faithful footballer-type who will love you and keep you for the rest of your life, then stop reading now. This isn't for you.

Firstly, that man doesn't exist – and this book is for smart girls with realistic expectations. The happy ending is a loser's fairytale reserved for the likes of Cheryl Cole and other head-in-the-sand types. It barely happens in the real world, let alone the crazy world of the Premiership. But a lot of young, carefree and happy girls are going through the football process and coming out the other side bitter, depressed and damaged (not to mention with a dose of some nasty-ass disease).

Date footballers, models, actors, or even those arty musicians if you must. I agree that it's all a thrill. (I wouldn't have done it if it wasn't.) But be wise about it and make it work for you. This world of VIP clubs and Premiership stars is ridiculous, so take a good look, laugh, enjoy – then get out while you still can!

The aim of this book is that its readers don't end up as just more bitter, forgotten conquests; more notches on a footballer's bedpost, who may try to get pregnant (or something equally stupid) in a desperate bid to entrap him. Instead, I am going to teach you how to work the whole footballer scene to your advantage. It's a dog-eat-dog world out there, and unless you use and abuse them, you *will be* used and abused. Be clever, be conniving, and be calculated. It may seem cold, but when you find yourself summoned to your beloved's solicitor's office, or hounded by a journalist eager to get that scoop, it pays to be prepared.

A FOOTBALLER IS FOR CHRISTMAS - NOT FOR LIFE!

I've written this as a handbook for the girl who might find herself entangled in the messy world of Premiership footballers. It's a full-on guide, packed with experience and advice I wish I'd had when I was in this situation. Since then, I've learned that a footballer is definitely just for Christmas – not for life. If you're to survive in a world where you might get stamped all over (just think of how painful those football studs would be – not to mention the stiletto heels of the other skanks), stop thinking about love and wise up. Otherwise you're going to get hurt in more ways than you ever thought possible.

Don't be disheartened if your new aim after reading this isn't to live your life in the pages of *OK* magazine, to always be on the 'right' side of a velvet rope, or to have a tack-tastic celeb wedding, and live in a future that's permanently orange. (Though I am totally pro-fake tanning, and I used to like the party pages at the back of *OK* – which seem to have slipped into a photo album for ex-*Big Brother* contestants.)

Fear not. For the life you once dreamed of is full of the constant fear of being replaced, not being as good as all those other wannabes, and your health being jeopardised by your unfaithful husband/boyfriend/illicit lover on an almost weekly basis.

Instead, congratulate yourself on being one of the smart ones. Rejoice as you embark on your journey through the tabloid world of pro footballers and exclusive clubs, and promise yourself that, while you're having fun, this is merely an adventure, *not* your whole life. The press may crassly term you a 'WAG wannabe', as they did to me and others – but in fact you're the complete opposite; you're now a WAG *don't*-wannabe.

Your sole aim is personal gain, whether in the form of life experience, notoriety, career advancement or financial security. It's up to you. Don't let anybody judge you for what you do. As Jesus said, "Let he who is without sin cast the first stone," and if every journalist who slated girls like Charlotte Meares and Rebecca Loos heeded that advice there would be no trashy stories depicting them in such a vile way.

Most of the girls I know who lived the life (myself included) have done it purely because it's fun – it's a game! When you're in a big city and you have big 'assets', meeting and dating guys is easy. Dating a Premiership footballer is just a fun way to up the ante. Girls like me don't want to settle

WAG Don't-Wannabe

down, we're not desperate to bag a baller, we're just having fun and enjoying the chase.

Another popular myth I'm keen to dispel is that we're all working-class girls with straightened hair and a loyalty card from our local tanning salon, as if all we want is to get some monetary benefit out of it. I know girls who live the life who have just got out of Stowe or Heathfield, or went to Edinburgh Uni purely for social schooling. They holiday in Mustique, St Moritz and Punta del Este, and dine at table three in E&O or Locanda Locatelli. Their bloodsteam is at least 60 percent Krug Grand Cuvée. They're educated and affluent – yet they will often receive a text which will get them running back to their old King's Road haunts:

"PH @ R – CD na"

This may look like it's been sent by a rather drunken friend, but what it really means is: Prince Harry (PH) at Raffles tonight (@ R) – Chelsy Davy not in attendance (CD na). These highly secretive texts are apparently sent out by friends of the Royals who, just like the footballers, want hot party girls to turn up and entertain the main man!

Similarly, Sloane Rangers may like to think that the football partying scene is reserved for 'train and tunnel' people and Eurotrash, but it spans the classes. As Cyndi Lauper once sang, "Girls just wanna have fun." No longer are Every House membership, daily breakfasts at Harry's and private yacht parties with Kate Moss in Ibiza enough – girls are competitive, and a secret affair with a Royal or an 'It boy' is just the thing to make them hot gossip among their peers that week.

3

But anyway, back to the guys we're all here for, the boys who have everything handed to them on a silver platter or in a silver bikini. The infamous Premiership footballers of Great Britain …

"Whether enjoying a quiet post-match spit roast or having a stunning young brunette with an unquenchable thirst for fame and questionable morals for a PA, the world of the high-profile football star is full of pitfalls."
– Steve Deane

I originally began writing this as therapy. I find it therapeutic to write about experiences which have elated me, devastated me, and everything else in between. I wanted to record what had happened with Wesley for the reader, but mostly for myself.

I realised, once I started writing, that although I knew through my experiences in London how some girls can deliberately pull a footballer with ease, I had never actually done so myself – nor, up until now, had I ever wanted to. But who am I to stand in the way of scientific research? This book didn't write itself you know!

From Wags to Bitches

I didn't like it when newspapers and magazines branded me a 'WAG wannabe' as I'm not. In fact nothing could be further from the truth. However, over the last few months I have temporarily become one of the girls they write about – with crazy results! Despite usually avoiding them like the plague, I have shamelessly gotten involved with quite a few footballers and the girls surrounding them: from spending a whole night grilling a well-known Premiership player about the way he treats women, to partying all weekend with the entire US national team whilst they qualified for the World Cup.

I went to footballer's parties at clubs, hotel after-parties with whole teams where we had to hide from coaches, and made many long, transatlantic phone calls to one of football's brightest rising stars. He was young, lonely, and he wouldn't leave me alone! I made the most of it by quizzing him on everything I could – all very discreetly, of course …

This insight has been invaluable to me. I feel I understand these strange creatures and their women more than ever before. Although some of the men I've encountered have been sweet, some naïve and many just plain dumb, they've all somehow reconfirmed in my mind what I knew about them all along.

I felt somewhat like a rather more glamorous Columbo, as I let certain players pursue me with phone calls and texts whereas I'd usually cut them dead. I slowly eked information out of them, like taking candy from a baby. One big player from Spain swore me not to use anything he told me in my book. I of course agreed … with my fingers crossed. But I'm not naming names. As you will see later, I've had my fair share of bad times with footballers' overpaid, egotistical lawyers, thank you very much. The last thing I need is Graham Shear banging at my door.[*]

If you're reading this book, the chances are you're one of the many thousands of pretty, educated girls in the UK who has thought about living the high life of a WAG. Then you've probably thought twice about it and felt really ashamed, vowing not to tell a soul. Who can blame you?

Maybe you've always wondered what it would be like to date a rich and famous footballer but have no connections. Maybe you're a huge fan of a certain player but have no idea how to make your dream of meeting him a reality. Or maybe, like me, you've met a footballer on the off-chance and want to know how to cope with what will inevitably become a precarious situation.

I guess there might be just a few of you out there who, like me, have already had relations with a footballer, feel bad about it and don't quite know quite which way to turn. You felt duped by him. You were bullied by his lawyers/agents/mother. You were sold out by the papers, and now you want to move on.

If so, I am an ally. Hopefully, a lot of this book will ring true to you and you can learn to laugh at it. Don't feel bad about wanting to gain something positive out of what might have ended unpleasantly and painfully. I'm not talking about money – quite the opposite. I never asked for anything from Wesley. I never saw any of his cash and I refused anything he offered me.

[*] *Graham Shear is one of football's biggest lawyers, usually at the epicentre of every scandal going.*

But when our farcical relationship took a serious downturn and almost turned my life upside down, I decided I deserved to get something out of all this. After all, it's not every day that one of England's top footballers falls into your lap. I would use it to my advantage – just as he had used me. I didn't want to do just a one-off kiss and tell, but I'd always wanted to write professionally. I'd done freelance copywriting when the chance arose, dabbled in PR and written for magazines, but my ultimate ambition was to write a book.

Throw in the scandal of a cheating footballer and a girl with ambition and here I sit – less than six months later, with a book deal. I've gained so much from Wesley without taking a penny from him.

Thanks to a hot and sweaty David Beckham in the 2002 World Cup and that tacky TV show, *Footballers' Wives*, there are a generation of young women now who think dating a player would be one of the greatest things in the world to do. But this once impressionable young girl has survived with only a (temporarily) broken heart and some bad press. (Please don't Google my name – promise me!)

Heed my advice. I wish I'd had this guide a year ago, for I could have used them to my advantage as much as they used me. Whatever your situation, I'm sure I've been there before. Luckily for you, I've made all the mistakes so that you don't have to.

WHO IS THE WAG DON'T-WANNABE?

*"It seems the fairer sex really do have the freedom
to do anything they want – just look at the inspirational
figure cut by Francesca Amber Sawyer."*
– Ian O'Doherty, *The Independent*

You may be wondering (as I often ask myself) why I am writing this book? Who am I? What makes me think I'm qualified to do this? Well, first of all, my name is Francesca Amber Sawyer (you may have gathered that already!) and I'm 23 years old. 'I Want to Know What Love Is' was at Number One when I was born, and I want Lucie Silvas' 'Forget Me Not' played at my funeral. You may have seen me about too, as I'm a self-confessed media whore.

The public's perception of me (as with most intelligent, and basically decent, girls in my situation – please stand up Rebecca Loos!) is pretty dire, and if they believe what they read they probably think I'm some ditzy, sluttish, bold-as-brass, talentless skank who needs to get a 'proper job'.

But I'm not a wannabe trying to live a life I can't afford, like all those tired features you see about girls wracked with debt trying to live a WAG's lifestyle on a cashier's budget. Thanks to my hard work I can live and shop independently, which gives me a greater feeling than any extravagant gift I've ever been given by a man. The house I share with friends in London, my car and even my boobs are all paid for by *moi* – and that's real independence to me, something nobody can take away from you.*

Like *Sex and the City* actress Kim Cattrall once said, "My life belongs to me, and that's a very sexy thing to own." So long as you've got the essentials covered and can comfortably and happily look after yourself, don't ever feel bad about letting a guy take you to St Tropez (you'd be silly to turn down a Nikki Beach opportunity) or buy you those darling Gina shoes in the Shoe Boudoir at Harrods you've been admiring.

I'm an old-fashioned girl at heart and so a man must always pay on a first date. (And the second, third, fourth, etc. You get the gist.) There's a big difference between *relying* on a man to get you by, and simply letting someone spoil you every now and then. Once you rely on somebody you may as well be a child again. Having to ask anybody to drive you somewhere, to buy you something or to do *anything* is something you should leave behind with your teens.

*Actually, I totally just remembered that I got my ex-boyfriend to pay for the second boob job, but it was just an upgrade. I paid for the initial pair so it doesn't count.

WAG Don't-Wannabe

I have always consciously aimed towards making my own money, so I've been careful with my spending. I bought my first horse, Lene, for just £50, from a part-time job collecting glasses at age fourteen. By the time I was eighteen I was working in the local nightclub whilst studying, and bought myself a beautiful, ginger Irish sports horse for £2,500 called Harvey, literally the Maybach of horses.

But I'm all down for reckless spending in the style of those to-die-for poolside tables at Nikki Beach, where everyone gets sprayed with £2,000 jeroboam bottles of Cristal. That is fun beyond belief, so long as some Eurotrash is paying. So remember, girls – the mint makes it first, it's up to you to make it last.

Workin' 9 to 5!

Features are my passion! I started writing for newspapers and magazines as a hard-up student, and it single-handedly paid for the upkeep of an extremely hungry horse – my beloved Harvey, the last tie to my childhood. (The amount of food he got through was enough to send me bankrupt.)

It was quick and easy money, and it beat working in my hometown's only nightclub, which I'll call the Island Club. The latter was a sticky-floored hole on Canvey Island run by a couple of carnies.* It was a place where middle-aged women, who had been coming there every weekend since they were old enough to drink, now frequented the club with their

* You know – circus folk!

own grown-up children. It made me want to get out of my small town and into the big city as fast as possible.

Anyway, since then I've written more stories than you can shake a stick at, ranging from 'My Boyfriend Has 14 Girl-friends' to a front-page exclusive for a national newspaper. I found that I could elaborate on any detail of my life, provided there was a quirky angle, and sell it to a magazine. What's more, most of it was even true – including the guy with fourteen girlfriends. He was a multibillionaire property developer, and for a time I lived in one of his many apartments on Park Lane. He loved to just go out, eat, drink, or go to clubs, and he gave me my first real insight into what London's all about.

Our relationship was never physical, but his relationships with some of his other thirteen girlfriends were. He really was London's answer to Hugh Hefner, and the three-storey, multimillion-pound apartment we lived in was like a British Playboy Mansion! The only thing different was that all his girls were dark-haired, natural beauties. I was the only blonde and, shall we say, 'enhanced' girl there. Some people thought our liaison was terrible, but I wouldn't take that time back for anything in the world.

Anyway, I digress.[*] I worked on features as I knew it was the best way to meet people in the industry and to gain insider knowledge. Through this I've managed to gain lots of work, and I'm now thinking about setting up my own company called Headline Hunters, to specialise in kiss-and-tells – from a more sympathetic angle, I might add.

* *You'll find I do this a lot!*

WAG Don't-Wannabe

Family, Friends, and Anything Else You Need to Know

"Treat your family like your friends, and your friends like family." – Anon

I've had a fantastic group of friends ever since I could walk and talk. There's something very magical about lifelong friends who love you for who you are, not because you can get them free vodka at the hottest club in town. I cherish every single one of them like a sister.

You usually take your family for granted, but with every passing year I discover something else that's truly remarkable about mine. My little family consisted of my mother, Cassandra, and father Clive. Mum was a redcoat back when Butlin's was cool, and eventually became quite a famous dancer in the swinging sixties. She had me later on in life and got ME into the bargain. It's been hard since, and I would love to have known her back when she was young and full of life. She sounds just like I am now. She gave up such a lot for my sister and I that I can only hope that, one day, I'll be able to repay her.

Dad's eight years younger than Mum, and originally from Germany. He totally looked like David Beckham when he was younger and loves the great outdoors. He and his brothers own a beautiful forest in Worthing, which we always used to camp in as children. Although I was happy, I was painfully shy. (I still am, in a way, now.) When I was eight they tried to get me out of this by buying me a dog. I spent the next few years furiously training, brushing, walking, talking about, even drawing that dog, and it did the trick. Whereas before I would never speak to my teachers, or rarely even other children (outside of my own couple of friends), I now chattered non-stop about my precious dog, showing them pictures and probably boring them senseless. He died just eight years after he came into my life, and I have felt severely cheated ever since.

Looking back though, I can see that everyone comes into your life for a reason – whether it's just for a good night or to truly touch your heart. And he did just that. He really was integral in making me the happier, more confident person I am today.

I'm also grateful for one of the best sisters ever to grace this earth. Anouska taught me everything I know, including PR skills which I learned during late-night lessons in bed. She is the original PR Princess! She gave up Essex and moved to Lincolnshire over a year ago now, which prompted me to do the same and to follow one of my biggest passions – London Town!

I love London and everything about it, but don't like to leave Zone One too often.* Some people may think that makes me a snob, but not so. I'm just a woman of extremes. When I was looking to move to London I wasn't interested in anywhere 'quiet', with 'room for parking' (or worse, a driveway!), that

---

* Uh, I now live in Zone Two, so perhaps I should take that back. If you look at the tube map though, it's totally fucked up. It's rectangular, so although Camden is far more central than Kensington it's still in Zone Two. I may write a letter to Boris Johnson to ask him to review the situation.

took a good fifteen-minute trek to get to the tube. I just don't see the point of living in London if you're going to be in a suburb. For me, it's all about living on a ridiculously busy road where I can get a taxi in ten seconds, mere minutes away from my favourite clubs, with a Nando's less than 300 steps away.

I recently moved from snooty Kensington to subcultural Camden, and it's incredibly busy! Even when I'm laying in bed, I can hear the hustle and bustle of traffic, tourists, revellers and music all seemingly vying for attention. Sometimes it feels like I'm at the centre of the world. (But isn't that Greenwich? Or is that just something to do with time?)

I also moved to London to write. To write about something, I have to live it and experience it – and so here I am. Camden isn't all Winehouse and crack-house, you know. It's actually got a very diverse literary background. My housemate pointed out that the house opposite was Charles Dickens' childhood home, and Mary Shelley was born here too. Surely it's got to rub off on me somehow?!

So, if you ever see me in town, in a bar, Grey Goose vodka, lemon and lime is my favourite drink. If you feel like asking me out, then Benihana, Nobu (only the Berkeley Square one) or Kensington Roof Gardens (which is beautiful in the summer) are my favourite restaurants.

(Did you hear what happened to their flamingos? I have a real thing for the birds after seeing wild flamingos in Madrid, but I heard that some ill-informed animal rights protesters got up into the roof gardens and hurled them over the edge of the building to set them free. What they didn't know was that the birds had their wings clipped, and the poor creatures fell to their deaths on Kensington High Street.)

But back to the point of this book. Through my penchant for partying in London, I've inadvertently found myself having an illicit relationship with one of England's best-known Premiership footballers, not to mention dalliances and brief encounters with a few others. Some were just casual flings; we met up very rarely, eventually becoming just friends. But my relationship with Wesley (remember Wesley? – return to your Man-Key!), and the reason for me writing this book, started with a chance meeting in a club, and escalated into a full-blown seven-month affair that broke both of our primary relationships – as well as my heart – into a million pieces.

That experience taught me a lot and and caused me a great deal of pain. (Which kind of goes against any tabloid 'ice-maiden bitch' image, don't you think?) I made a good few stupid mistakes, but soon learned how to look after myself via the agents, the high-powered media lawyers, the journalists desperate to get their scoop and the ruthless footballers themselves. Unfortunately, I also learned that, no matter how much your relationship meant to you, with the help of a lawyer anything and anyone can be made to 'disappear'.

I finally decided to end the relationship with Wesley and turn what was fast becoming a horrible experience into something more positive. If all of you girls out there wised up and kicked some serious footballer ass into touch, there would be no need to be a so-called 'victim' anymore. Kiss-

and-tell stories are no longer just basic black and white portrayals of him as the stud/love rat and her as the poor victim/dirty slut, depending on how the editor feels that day. So to all the have-been and would-be victims – fight back!

Getting involved with a famous footballer in this country can be soul-destroying; it can even break you if you're not careful. But if you take it all with a pinch of salt it can be more fun than you imagine, and makes watching *Match of the Day* so much more exciting. So heed my advice, put on those fabulous Gina shoes and go forth with confidence ...

WAG DON'T-WANNABE – ORIGINS OF THE SPECIES

"She should feel privileged Ashley Cole was
sick in her car." – Ashley Cole

The title of this book may seem a little odd to you. Lots of people have asked me what the heck it means, but I think that the above quote, from *The Sun*, sums up perfectly my disdain for egotistical footballers.

I have been called, on many occasions, a 'WAG wannabe' – a term I detest and wholly reject in equal measure. I've seen many girls stuck with the same label, including Danielle Lloyd (definitely not a wannabe – she's doing it her way!), and there are a whole community of girls (I use the term 'community' lightly, as not all of us get on) who are both party-loving and hard-working, and can see that being associated with a footballer might do their careers no end of good.

Despite all this, we still get stuck with the same sad tag.

Hence my title of 'WAG don't-wannabe', the name I've made up for exactly the sort of girls I'm talking about. They're strong, they're real, and they don't give a damn what anyone says! Their aspirations go beyond marrying someone for money – unlike most delusional WAGs – and they usually have some master-plan behind their dazzling smile

That's the difference, you see. Don't-wannabes will have a fling or a date because it's fun, it's a thrill, and it might even further their aims. But they are ultimately morally sound girls who aspire to marry for love and commitment, something they know that you can't get from a player. (And yes, I mean 'player' in every sense of the word.)

The tabloids depict the 'WAG-wannabes' as looked down on by the WAGs. But in reality, the don't-wannabes are really disappointed by the WAGs as members of the female gender. They're the ones who are sacrificing their lives, their wedding fingers and even their wombs for these cheating men. For don't-wannabes it's fun for now; for the WAGs it's *for life*. That's quite a sad and scary prospect when you think about it, isn't it?

Why Would Anybody Want to Date a Footballer?

"Congratulations to Wayne Rooney. He scored three times on Tuesday. He hasn't done that since he gate-crashed a pensioners' bingo night." – Jonathan Ross

WAG Don't-Wannabe

"If I was spotted with someone famous, my name would fly straight into the papers. That's the way the industry works now." – Cassie Sumner

With hindsight, I ask myself the above question on a daily basis. Then I remember the thrills and spills of my experiences and realise they weren't all bad – in fact some of them were good, so damn good that I felt compelled to write about them.

That aside, however, there's a business-minded aspect to it. What with every newspaper and magazine in Britain clamouring to give WAGs their own highly-paid columns, plus features on what they're wearing, who they're seen with or where they're going, it's easy to see the appeal: endless rounds of shopping; a limitless credit card; everything handed to you on a plate. Fame and Fortune remain the age-old ambitions. But in the past, you would have had to possess a rather amazing talent for singing, dancing or acting in order to achieve them, and even then you weren't guaranteed success. But by having a footballer on your arm, all this and more can be yours.

Try these examples for size, they'll make you as sick as a dog – a.k.a. Carole Malone of the *Sunday Mirror*, when she found out Abi Titmuss was a millionaire through paparazzi image sales alone, or Posh, when she realised Rebecca Loos was hotter, fitter *and* more intelligent:

"Dating a footballer has helped so many models."
– Cassie Sumner

EXAMPLE ONE: You can struggle as an aspiring model for years, go to endless castings and spend fortunes on agents and portfolios. But why, when you can get yourself a footballer and then you too, like the dumpy-but-lovely Coleen, can end up with a lavish ten-page spread in *Vogue*?

Please do not take this as a criticism of Coleen. She's the first to recognise and admit that she's not classic supermodel material. If she were in the real world of modelling, she wouldn't even make it onto a regular agency's books because she's not skinny enough and definitely not tall enough.

Sad but true. She's even made a TV show centred on this concept called *Coleen's Real Women*, which gives regular women off the street a chance to model for a national fashion campaign. It's a brilliant concept, and clearly she's aware of both how fickle the market is and how lucky she is, and is using her popularity to change things. That gets a big don't-wannabe thumbs up from me.

Abby Clancy and Danielle Lloyd fit into this same category. Let me ask you a question: which other contestants can you name from the show *UK's Next Top Model*? Tick tock, tick tock … None? Well, that's the right answer. And which other previous Miss Englands can you name? Right again – none! (If you can, you're either a personal friend or relative of theirs or an obsessive stalker who needs to be locked away from young women.)

My point: they are the only contestants who went on to become successful afterwards; so what do they have in common? That's right – they both dated footballers! The golden ticket!

They probably weren't the best models in either show. In fact I'm pretty sure that neither of them won, but they're certainly more successful than whoever beat them! Ditto, who are the single most publicised members of five-piece girl groups the Spice Girls and Girls Aloud respectively? They just happen to be Victoria Beckham and Cheryl Cole.

What. A. Coincidence.

EXAMPLE TWO: Go to university, study to be a journalist when you could be having fun instead, spend years thanklessly making cups of tea at a local rag whilst looking forward to the pinnacle of your career – covering the annual local fete. Or, date a footballer and get offered your own weekly column (read: double page spread) in a national newspaper or weekly glossy.

We've all seen this happen, much to the annoyance of columnists like Carole Malone. She hates those guys, and quite rightly so. She's worked for years to become a successful writer and she sees women with little-to-no writing talent coming up through the ranks faster than the office whore. She's openly admitted that she resents their success – while I'll always be the first to defend those girls who, like Abi Titmuss, work the media game to their advantage with such spectacular results.

Practically anyone can get their own column, or call themselves an author, these days, so long as they've got a goal-scorer in their beds. Just look at me! I would never have been paid to write this book if I hadn't had the inside scoop and a unique perspective. It must make professional journalists like Carole heave, but if that's what the public wants, that's what they'll continue to get.

EXAMPLE THREE: Struggle as a little-known designer for years and never get anywhere, because it's *who* you know, not what you know, in the fashion world. Or – yes, you guessed it – date a member of the Premiership and you've got yourself a tasteless clothing line in a top high street store of your choice, complete with sequin and animal print designs which will be bought by chavs across the country. People will queue around the block on the date of the launch and everything will sell out in minutes, because everyone wants a slice of your life. But there's a hefty price tag to pay. Soon the items will make their way onto eBay, and then onto the hunched backs of those gormless individuals who think less of design than of which WAG has put her name to it.

(I can safely say that, apart from a Kelly Brook bikini I bought in a moment of elation after my breast enlargement, I've never bought a celebrity-endorsed item of clothing. The bikini was a hideous, polka-dotted, frilly number and I've never even worn it. I feel so much better about myself now.)

Players and Princes

I've worked out a theory which I call Players and Princes. The hype that surrounds footballers and their WAGs has turned into a phenomenon in this country, where more girls would rather marry a little-known Premiership player (of which there are hundreds) than Prince William. While there are more players than princes, there's still one little problem. There are still only so many footballers, definitely not enough to go around. (Although, in my experience, the way they get through girls makes it seem like they're trying to make up for it.)

I find that with men you're looking to date, the two most important attributes come down to: 1. Hotness; 2. Wealth/Power. Normally, one must be sacrificed to the other to a greater or lesser degree.

I've dated many a rich and/or powerful man who has been lacking in the looks department. I once dated a guy from New York who was often in London on business. He was lovely, took me to the nicest places and often did the nicest things for me. Once I was really upset over a personal crisis, and had been living in the Hilton hotel for about a month, which is not nearly as glamorous as it sounds.

Anyway, he knew I had some kind of obsession with orange Fanta, a bit like Kel on *Keenan and Kel*, and so one day he got his long-suffering PA to fill my suite with Fanta creations! A tower of cans, a pyramid of cans ... you get the theme. It's one of the sweetest things anyone's ever done for me. (Literally, in terms of sugar content.) HOWEVER – due to the logistics of the above rule, he was of course hideously overweight and slightly balding. His only six-packs were rolls of fat, or bank notes in multiples thereof.

On the other hand, I've dated some *fiiiine* hotties too, who mostly sleep all day and party all night, one being a worldly Parisian boy who came to live in London. He had model good looks (almost *too* good looking), the body of a Greek god and a cracking personality. His flaw? Well, he was a no-strings traveller and thus a pauper. He left school and didn't pursue any further education, drifting from job to job, which he never held down as he was too pretty to know how to work hard. We spent a long, hot summer together and, although it was incredibly exciting, romantic and spontaneous, at the grand old age of 22 I wondered where he would be in ten years time. I could imagine that, if we ever married, I'd have to become a barefooted street urchin who joins the Hare Krishna gang for free food in order to follow him tirelessly across the globe.

I almost don't know which is worse – to marry the rich-but-fat guy who repulses you, or to be an impoverished mother of ten with the hot-yet-poor boy.

And this is where footballers come in. Not only are they incredibly young, hot, fit – I could go on – but they also have the wealth not usually associated with young, hot fitties. (Apart from toffs but they don't count. While they're okay in deafening Boujis, once you can hear them drone on about "Mummy and Daddy's house in Mustique" and their "cracking good time in Gstaad last Christmas – oh, you have to go! We spent all day at the Eagle Club!", you just want to take a sawn-off shotgun to their face.)

Thus, in conclusion, for the average girl a footballer really does appear to have it all.

DING! "YOU'RE DONE!" – GET THE LOOK

*"I'm so fricking pissed. I went to get my brows done
and I told her to make me look like J-Lo. And then that
fricking Russian toad made me look like Liza Minnelli."*
– White Chicks (2004 movie)

Good news! I actually don't think that appearance is the be-
all and end-all in acquiring the attention of a footballer.
Take a look at the WAGs of some Premiership footballers;
they're all attractive, well groomed and presentable, but
they're often not the most beautiful women in the country. I
will always remember when I was in the offices of a national
Sunday newspaper and getting on quite well with the features
editor. He had agreed (under duress!) to show me pictures of
Wesley's live-in girlfriend.

For all the months I'd been in the affair, I'd stupidly
believed that I loved him and couldn't understand why he

wouldn't leave her for me. It was soul-destroying to imagine what amazing qualities she must have had that I couldn't quite live up to. I was constantly imagining some Gisele-like Amazonian goddess, whose impossibly beautiful aspects forced me into accepting I was second best. His bit on the side. His mistress. His dirty little secret.

You cannot even begin to imagine my shock (and jubilation!) when I saw that she was, in fact, a short, slightly chubby chav. She had her dirty brown hair scragged back into a Croydon facelift (okay, we all do sometimes, at Primark or the gym – but this picture was taken at a party in Embassy, for God's sake!), funny crooked teeth, acres of pasty sallow skin, and a look about her that suggested her ancestors engaged in a little incest.

Okay, maybe I'm being a little cruel, and I'm a horrible, horrible person for judging her solely on her looks, which is something I don't approve of usually. And yes, it's sad to admit it, but it made me feel so much better about myself. It also made me realise that it wasn't a case of not being good enough for Wesley – it was just that I would always be 'the mistress'. Somehow, crazily, it made the whole thing easier to accept.

Having been around footballers and the girls that they date, have affairs with or simply shag, I can tell you that the looks the majority go for are not dissimilar from your average builder. (Or the average caveman, probably.)

Whilst the sheikhs, businessmen and blue-blooded party boys I've known and dated have appreciated the fashion-forward, discreet yet label-laden looks reminiscent of Audrey Hepburn in *Breakfast at Tiffany's*, footballers just don't get it. They want, quite simply, tits and ass. Go for some high heels, a tiny dress and pretend the word 'subtlety' never existed. Multiply the depth or volume of everything from your hair to your tan by at least five and you're good to go!

You rarely find a footballer dating some obscure filmmaker, artist or haute couture fashion-model type with strong features, a flat chest and a quirky cropped hairstyle. What (based on my observations) they do go for is the tanned glamour-model prototype who isn't overly upper class or a high-flying career woman. Maybe that's because most footballers (see the use of 'most' there!) come from modest backgrounds and their tastes are not dissimilar from your average builder. Make use of this and try to conceal as best you can your classic dress sense, properly enunciated vowels, good education and aspirations.

Plastic Fantastic!

"I definitely believe in plastic surgery. I don't want to be an old hag, there's no fun in that." – Scarlett Johansson

Girls, if you're anti-surgery then good for you! Please skip to page 38.

For my own part, although I hate to say it – and I kind of disagree with myself about it – I am totally pro-surgery. If you have a flat chest, you can work it in the Paris Hilton fashion and learn to love it. But if you're really unhappy with it, you can change it. We're living in an age where these things are possible, and I believe we would be letting science down if we didn't take advantage of its advances in the medical field.

Liposuction, on the other hand, I am dead against. Get off your fat arse, join a gym and sweat the fried chicken out through your pores! Lipo is never the answer, it's gross, you can be left bumpy and scarred and ... did I mention that it's *gross*?

One time I went to St Tropez for a party, and one of the girls in our group was quite skinny but had hideous scars on the backs of her knees that only got lighter as she tanned. They were from lipo! As far as I'm aware, you don't get scars from losing weight at the gym. What did the mums of Kanye West and Cher in the film *Clueless* both die from? Follow me? Just promise that you won't have lipo. Good, let's continue.

Although I am totally pro-breast implants/uplifts, etc, I feel slightly different about facial surgery which actually changes the way *you* look. I think you need to think long and hard about any fundamental changes you make. That face is YOU. It represents hundreds of years of congenital heritage and evolution. It shows your roots, your biological makeup, your ethnicity – everything! It's good to be slightly quirky, but in a way that you're comfortable with. I have a slightly posh upturned nose. I've battled for years with the question of whether I want to change it or not. But when I've mentioned it to men-friends in the past (including two who openly offered to pay for boob jobs, being totally pro-plastic) they were horrified, telling me it was what gave my face character. So it's up to you. If it's quirky and comfortable, stay with it. But if it's making you depressed and withdrawn, then plastic surgery could be the best thing you ever did.

When I bought myself a boob job for my 21st birthday, shortly afterward my life began to change incredibly. That's what started me writing my *Essex Girl in London* blog, with the opening chapter titled 'Can 600CCs of Silicone Really Change Your Life?' Carry on, dear reader, and know that it can:

The year 2006 – I turned 21 and decided to change my life – I was going to ... save the world? Travel to Africa to fight the AIDS epidemic? No – I was going to get a boob job.

You see I've thought about this for as long as I could remember – if only I wasn't so afraid of needles, if only I had the money etc ... So after years of wanting and wishing I finally decided enough was enough. It was the summer of 2004, I had finished college and sold my horse, my beloved Harvey, the last token of being young and free. Long gone were the days of dossing off college to go to the pub, drinking on week nights and riding round the beach all day – as I breathed in his horsy leathery smell for the last time I realised it wasn't just a horse I was letting go of, it was my childhood. Bring it on!!

... As my friends were getting into debt with overdrafts and loans and credit cards (the thought of a credit card makes me shudder) I was secretly stacking up a pile of cash for 'The Op'.

My first year of work was harsh. Long hours, long commute, hard work, and a lot of blagging! After six months a new PA was brought in to work 'alongside' me – alongside my ass! More like trample on top of me, and jump on me until I am nothing but DUST. The girl knew nothing and being almost ten years my senior had to act as if she knew it all. Of course she didn't and to cut a long blog short I spent the next six months or so crying every day at the unfairness of it all.

I had tried confronting her straight on, everything – nothing worked. Apparently if you're only 20, blonde and from Essex you're always the dumbest in the room. Finally one day I snapped. I quit my job with just enough money in my bank for The Op, some good experience and a lot of relief to be out of the situation. I decided there and then that this was the point to have The Op. If I could walk out of my job with no fear (OK there was a little fear and I did call some well-known employment agencies the minute I was out the door) then I could do this. I know that people say if you expect surgery to change your life then you will be disappointed but I definitely haven't been. It's like when they cut me open on that table they didn't just put silicone in there – they implanted a mojo too!

100 percent Silicone, 100 percent Fabulous

"If a man's looking anywhere except my chest he's looking at another man." – Dolly Parton

WAG Don't-Wannabe

So how do you go about it? Well, it's good to research lots of different companies and surgeons, see their work and judge what you like best. One of the best ways to find a good surgeon is by word of mouth. On the London party scene every second girl has fakies, so your best bet is to simply go ahead and ask them the name of their surgeon. They shouldn't be offended (at least I've never found it to be the case); in fact they should really be flattered that you like the work enough to want the same yourself.

I found my surgeon totally by chance. I'd been looking at a clinic in Cyprus because ... well, to be honest it was because it was cheap. I only had £3,000 and so didn't really have enough money to get it done in the UK. It wasn't going to stop me! I found my lovely surgeon, Dr Andreas Skaparis, and took a liking to him straightaway from what I read.

Okay, so maybe I didn't exactly practice what I preach there, but I have really good instincts about people. You should *not* employ instinct alone when choosing the man to perform life-changing surgery on you. I was silly – but ultimately lucky!

Andreas has an office in Harley Street, central London – the mothership of all things plastic. I went along with my sister the first time, and even got her to come into his office with me, which I soon regretted. I had to get topless and have pictures taken. It seems that whenever I'm in a doctor's surgery, about to have something painful or embarrassing done, Anouska is always there behind the curtain, trying to stifle her laughs.

I remember, not long ago, I had bleeding ... from somewhere you don't want to bleed from. (I'm only sharing this with you because you paid £7.99 for the book. If you got this from a library, skip the page. Stingy.) For days I began to imagine all sorts of awful things, like colon cancer, bowel cancer, all kinds of cancer, and so upon my sister's advice took the first appointment I could get at my local doctor's surgery. I took her along for moral support; the prospect of having to show my chafed a-hole to a room full of medics wasn't one I relished.

The inevitable moment came. Behind a flimsy curtain (with, ahem, *cracks* in it), in the manner of Russell Brand I had to "pull down my trousers and pants" and show them what was going on. This was *way* too intimate for my liking. It turned out that I had an anal tear (ouch!), so I was questioned about my sexual exploits and whether I had anal sex. My sister, meanwhile, was desperately trying but failing to conceal her laughter as I tried to explain and defend myself.

(As it happens, I've never had anal sex. It's just not right. I once knew this girl who had to have a colostomy bag from the age of 20, and I heard a horror story involving a tomato skin once. I would rather die than take the chance of that happening to me, even though I don't eat tomatoes.)

Back to Dr Skarparis' office. I'm topless behind a screen, he's having a poke about and my sister is craning her neck to have a look. Despite all the embarrassing nakedness I like him and his surgical group, so I book the surgery for that April in Larnaca, Cyprus.

I know what you're going to say. "You had surgery abroad?!!?" But honestly, all those 'sun, sand and surgery' horror stories you see in magazines are rare cases. Not only that, but Cyprus has no MRSA which is a big pro these days. Yes, we want bigger boobs, but we don't want to end up like poor Leslie Ash. No court payout can get her normal lips (uh, I mean her pre-MRSA state of health) back.

Who Cares?

You may resent having to pay for a loved one to have a 'free holiday', but trust me, it's anything but. Your designated carer has to carry your cases,* get you to and from the clinic and help out whilst you're in hospital, as the nurses are run off their feet. When you're back from your surgery, they help you in and out of bed, to the toilet, to the shower when you can (you can't get your stitches wet for seven days) and to get dressed. It's not all lounging around the pool, sipping cocktails.

It's also worth thinking long and hard about who your carer should be. Never choose a boyfriend unless you have a very close relationship and you don't mind him witnessing you look and smell like a dog's arse. You can't even lift your arm to brush your hair, makeup is the last thing on your mind and you can't shower for almost a week. For these reasons it's best to take someone who has to love you unconditionally,

* I really just mean on the way home, when you're not allowed to lift anything. But hell, if you're paying for them, why not make them your bitch for the week and get them to carry everything for you at all times?

regardless of what you look like – like a mother or sister. Male relatives are a big no-no, as you spend a large amount of time with your baps out and/or talking about them. This can make things a mite uncomfortable for all concerned for many years to come.

Choose somebody who is not selfish or lazy. Carry out a secret test whilst at home. Pretend you've hurt your back and you can't get out of bed. Ask for a drink and, if they bring it quickly with ice and a slice, they're on board. If they're tardy or just plain ignore you, they're out!

You usually have your surgery on the first or second day to give you maximum recovery (and tanning!) time. It's a complete fallacy that you can't fly after a boob job in case your implants explode. (I think this happened back in the seventies, when techniques were nowhere as sophisticated as they are now.) If you have silicone cohesive gel, they will never leak either.

I tested the latter theory when I got my first set of implants back after my second op. I'd even put them on eBay and publicised it in a national newspaper to raise funds for the op. (This was due to a little misunderstanding with my now-ex-boyfriend as to who would be paying for it. As soon as he saw the article in the *Daily Sport* it was soon rectified!) I put one of the implants under the leg of a chair and sat on it – nothing happened! So I'm quite confident they're only as vulnerable as the rest of my body – or maybe less so, as I'm sure I'd die if you put a chair leg on my chest and sat on it. But my implant would most definitely remain intact!

Will you have the implant under or over the muscle? If you're squeamish ... get over it and keep reading – you have to be able to read about it if you're going to do it! That's right, in breast augmentation surgery they *cut* your muscle! The benefits of having the implant under the muscle, as I did, are that it has a more natural look as the outline is hidden by a layer of muscle and fat. You'll still be able breastfeed perfectly normally as your breast, as it was pre-surgery, is still intact. The downside is that it's bloody painful and takes longer to get over.

If you want that Victoria Beckham-style, fake, stuck-on look then go for over the muscle. The outline of the implant is a lot more defined, as it's literally right under the skin. If you have saggy or larger breasts to begin with, this might be an option for you. It's a lot less painful and is quicker to recover from.

Please Cut Here ✄

Where do you want your incision? I, like many other people, have it in the crease beneath the breast, which is the obvious place. As they naturally hang down a bit you can't even see it, and the scar itself is only about five centimetres long.

Breast implants need to be renewed on average every ten to fifteen years. Think of this when first having them done. It's not a one-off payment you'll be making – they need to be maintained for life. When I heard this when I was younger it really put me off. But now, having had two operations within two years, I can tell you that, pain and money-wise, it's been worth it ten times over and is definitely the best decision I ever made. People always ask me if I have any regrets about having surgery. My only regret is that I didn't do it sooner.

Crowning Glory

> *"Gentlemen prefer blondes."* – Andrew Mellon
> *"My hair is a powerful construction aided by static,
> hairspray and willpower. In man-hours it's
> comparable to the pyramids."* – Russell Brand

Your hair should be your crowning glory. Men tend to like it long, shiny and healthy. It has to be touchable. Long, tumbling locks just make men think of tumbling around in bed with you. Have it highlighted and be a power-blonde. It's a well-known fact that blondes have more attention paid to them. It's said that, in ancient times, they evolved in a bid to stand out amongst all the brunettes and gain a mate.

I also read somewhere that some men were shown a picture of the same woman; in one she had blonde hair; in the other she had brown – almost all the men felt more physically attracted to the blonde picture, rated her attractiveness higher, and said the blonde was younger, even slimmer!*

We're really just applying that same theory here. If you're naturally dark and it suits you to be brunette, stick with it – it looks great! I sometimes wish that I could revert to being

* *Evidently it's the men that are the dumb ones here, not the blondes!*

38

brunette, but I just don't get away with it very well. I did it once when I was about 20 and was featured in *Nuts* magazine with my sister, who's also a brunette. I hated that picture so much that it forced me back to the bleach! Yes, it was low-maintenance and my hair was healthier, but when I went out I felt almost invisible – and that I *do not* like!

It's worth remembering that men almost always cheat with girls who have longer hair than their primary partner. (The bastards! That's not my opinion – that's a *fact*.) Longer hair, according to evolutionary theory, represents youth and fertility – so get growing! If you're like me, and find growing your hair really hard, don't despair. There is plenty you can do to ensure optimum hair growth. Eat a healthy diet that includes a hair supplement containing vitamins and minerals. You can also have regular scalp massages which stimulate the follicles, or regularly use saunas and steam rooms, where the heat will increase circulation, making both hair and nails grow stronger and faster.

Hair growth isn't all about the roots; it's in the ends too. Due to excessive heat styling and lots of washing, ends can become weak, split and break off, making your hair shorter. If you have blonde hair which is regularly highlighted, then this is all the more likely to occur due to bleach drying the hairs out.

If this is the case then it's up to you to prevent it with hair treatments. Some of the best are in an oil form and work with heat. One trick is to cover your hair in treatment oil and then go sit in the sauna or steam room for up to 20 minutes. The heat will open all your pores and hair shafts, allowing the oil to penetrate deep inside.

After washing your hair, try to always use a deep conditioner for dry/damaged/coloured hair as these are the most nourishing. As many times a week as you can, leave conditioner on your hair for a good hour or so whilst you do other things, like paint your nails or read a book. Your hair will thank you for it.

Banish the hairdryer from your life. (Well, for at least six days a week anyway.) Make a pact with yourself that you will only blow-dry your hair once a week. If you style it with heated tongs or straighteners, then you don't even need to blow-dry it. Try to keep straightening and heat-styling to a minimum too, restricting it to nights out or important dates. The rest of the time, let your hair dry naturally overnight in a large, loose plait. When you wake up in the morning your hair will be tousled in loose waves, perfect for our boho era and kind on your tresses too.

When you're going out, the sky is the limit with your hair. (I mean that both figuratively and in terms of its physical height!) Hair is the one thing that makes you really stand out, so try different looks. Quiffs are in and can be really flattering, but beware – avoid them if you have a large forehead, as they can look dodgy in photos. Instead of the usual straight look, try putting your hair into two plaits and running the straighteners down both of them two or three times. The look is loose, tousled locks that don't look too 'done'. On the other hand, you can use your straighteners as curling irons and add extensions for the length that curled hair lacks. Just remember my golden rules for curling hair:

1. Be sure it's what you really want to do. Once you start there's no going back, as re-straightening curly hair wrecks it beyond belief. You may as well wash your hair in talcum powder and blow-dry it thrice a day. Curling is high-maintenance, so be sure before you go for it.

2. Don't make like Shirley Temple with a head full of ringlets, unless you want to look like the aforementioned child star or a Victorian hooker. Start to curl from the mid-lengths, or even just curl the ends of your hair underneath. This give a much better result, is kinder to your hair and allows more length.

3. Don't curl every last scrap. Do it randomly and loosely, almost as if you were a bit drunk. If you find this hard, a bottle or two of wine should produce the desired effect. Let the hair that frames your face, especially any fringe, stay natural. Don't straighten it, as this will look hideously chavvy (straightened fringe with curled-to-death hair is *not* the look you're going for), but let it graduate easily into your waves.

4. Use extensions to lengthen and fill out your hair. Buy only 100 percent human hair and weave two colours together for a more natural look. Buying extensions that look truly natural is one of the hardest things in the world to do (other than bringing peace to the Middle East, perhaps, or finding a prospective husband in Faces). In order to do it right, you

need a very helpful shop assistant and a friend on hand whose interests are not commission-based. Try out the colours next to your own hair in both artificial and natural daylight. If you have your hair regularly highlighted or lowlighted, it can be harder still as your colour changes subtly every six weeks or so. Once you get the colours right though, they can look fantastic! As the extensions are made from human hair, you can wash and curl them as you would your own. Curl the extensions from the mid to end lengths as they will be going underneath most of your own natural hair, and clip in evenly throughout.*

5. Use serum and a shine spray on the finished work to get rid of any frizz and bouffant-ness (yes, that *is* a word – as of now!) and twist individual curls around serum-coated fingers to define and relax.

6. Use two mirrors so you can get a good look at the back of your head. You would be surprised at the amount of girls I see around who clearly think that, just because they can't see the back of their head, no one else can. Check that there's nothing crazy going on, like a random straight chunk or an extra-long extension flying about. Don't trust a friend to tell you. They may not be as precise as you are, as no one cares about your own hair more than you. They may just say it looks great to get you out of the door, but the mirror doesn't lie. Trust the mirror.

---

* *Make sure no one strokes your head like a dog – they will think you have some hideous bumpy scalp disease from the extension clips. Pull any wandering hands away immediately. Likewise, if you're planning on staying out, accept that you're going to be doing a walk of shame the next morning with a handful of hair, as if you've killed a cat.*

WAG Don't-Wannabe

"I think the most important thing a woman can have –
next to talent, of course – is her hairdresser."
– Joan Crawford

Getting the right cut and colour can take years to perfect, via many salons, stylists, hats and tears along the way. Luckily, after having it 'razored' by my next-door neighbour for years, then being a model for free highlights at the hairdressing school while I was a student, my hair finally found its guardian angel. I stumbled across Andrea one day when I asked a girl I'd seen in the street with really cool hair where she had it done. And so she led me to the hair guru!

Andrea operated out of a small salon in my Essex hometown. It had been there since time began, but I'd never stopped to notice. She really listened to what I wanted and, before I knew it, I was the proud owner of the best highlights I've ever had. She goes right to the root, which is rare in most highlighters, and gets the colour perfect every time. The women of Canvey Island are incredibly lucky to have her.

I try to get my highlights done every six weeks, and mark it in my diary so that I know exactly when I last had it done. Every second or third time I get some lowlights put in to break up the blonde, and a couple of times a year I have a whole head done to freshen up the colour. Brunettes, you're probably thoroughly bored by now, but thank your lucky stars you don't have to go through this! I have to say though – being a blonde is definitely worth it.

Terracotta Temptress – Secrets of the Perfect Tan

"Oh my God, Karen. You can't just ask people why they're white." – Gretchen, Mean Girls (2004 movie)

Don't bother with sun-beds to gain that WAG-tastic tan – fake it the easy way! I'm not a huge fan of fake tan and can't remember the last time that I used it. I use a very simple little product instead: Sun Shimmer. That's right, those £2.49 bottles with the modest Rimmel label that you see in your local chemist's. It's basically makeup for your body, so you apply it with a special mitt when you're going for a night out and wash it off the next day! You can get a seriously deep golden glow from these products and it takes a little over ten minutes to tan your whole body.

Of course, you can cheat and only tan the parts of you that are showing. But beware, reader – I did this once when I was in a rush to go to a big party. It was being held by an ex-*Big Brother* contestant (I know, I know, but it was fun, okay?) in a penthouse suite at the Lanesborough Hotel. I thought I was rather clever in only tanning my legs and arms, as I danced away in my little black dress. It was only much later when I realised that, having decided to strip down to my underwear and dance on a table, I hadn't tanned my stomach or chest and looked like a pigmentation-challenged sideshow freak! Never mind, I'm sure they weren't looking at my skin tone anyway. The point is that, although I enjoy a little tanning in St Tropez or Ibiza in the summer, I'm not ageing my body and face beyond repair on a weekly basis for anybody! Just fake it, girls, don't bake it!

If you need something a little more long-lasting and substantial than what is essentially body makeup, then I'm sure there are hundreds of great fake tanners out there. Faking a golden glow in less than a day – when your friend has just come back from Barbados, where she fried for two weeks to get the same colour as you – can be very satisfying.

Sometimes though, particularly in the middle of winter when your naked skin is almost blue, there's nothing better than the feeling of warm sun. Although I preach against frying yourself week-in/week-out for that amber traffic light look, I do indulge in a little recreational sunbathing when the chance arises. My annual summer holiday is a week of basking like a cat in the sunshine, whipping off everything except the smallest bikini bottoms I can get away with. But as with everything, it's about moderation. If you were fully-baked all year round you just wouldn't appreciate it when it was summertime. When baking, just ensure that you wear a moisturising sun protector, cover your lips with a high-factor shield and wear big sunglasses to protect your eyes, preventing crow's feet. No squinting allowed!

Work It Out

"I laugh a lot. It burns lots of calories."
– Jessica Simpson

One thing I definitely recommend investing in is a health club membership. I never used to worry about my weight; it seemed I could eat what I liked and do no exercise and still stay a svelte size eight. However, if you're out drinking all night most weeks, it soon takes its toll. Because you don't see the changes yourself, you don't realise it, but trust me – it's affecting your looks.

As going out to clubs and drinking are part of your party-girl lifestyle, you must take action to counteract its effects. The gym is the perfect place for this. My health club membership is £72 a month, but it's worth every penny. Just paying the fee makes me feel healthier. You don't even need to break into a sweat anymore – gyms have advanced! Take the Power Plate, for example: this wonder machine gives you the effect of a hard hour's workout in just ten to twenty minutes, via your holding different poses. Genius! It also has a massage function, which is one of the only proven ways of eradicating the vodka-loving girl's worst nightmare – cellulite. I just lay myself across it in different positions for about five minutes and, after a few weeks, it really does make a difference. (I also exercise there, of course, as well as taking full advantage of the spa facilities.)

Steam rooms and saunas are incredibly good for your skin, and are worth having at least twice a week if you can manage it. One little trick I have is to shower and work a hot oil treatment into my wet hair – I then go in the sauna, or steam room (or both!), for as long as I can bear (up to twenty minutes each) before washing it out. The effect of the heat on the oil is amazing. Your hair will be transformed into silky swathes quick-sharp, perfect for those bleach blondes like myself whose stressed-out hair needs all the help it can get. Saunas and especially steam rooms are also excellent for your skin. As someone once said to me, "A shower rinses your skin, a steam rinses your pores." It's great as it brings all your spots, blackheads and any other problems to the surface. (For this reason it's worth remembering that, if you have a big party coming up, you may want to avoid the steam or sauna for at least a few days beforehand, to prevent an outbreak.)

Saunas are used by boxers to sweat out excess weight in water so that they can move down a class in weight. This is reason enough to go sweat it out in one! Once you get used to the stifling heat it can become very therapeutic – especially in the colder winter months – and you begin to see great improvements in your skin, hair and general wellbeing.

Let's not forget one other important reason for going to the gym – to check out the hot guys! This can be a great motivation when you're dying of boredom on the treadmill or some other hideously tedious machine – just watch some hottie pumping iron and the minutes pass in a flash. Another good way to make time pass, and take your mind off your erratically beating heart, is to take stock of your life in your head. Make plans, whether it's what you want to wear that night or your life goals for the year ahead. Gym time is good thinking time.

Remember to vary your workouts to keep them stimulating for both mind and body. When you go swimming, try to up the amount of lengths you do each time. At other times, concentrate solely on the Power Plate or some intense uphill walking on the treadmill. Lots of health clubs hold dance classes and yoga too, which can be a fun way to mix things up.

The Illustrated Girls

> *"I want to get a tattoo of myself on my*
> *entire body, only two inches taller."*
> – Steven Wright

Tattoos used to be reserved for rebellious teenagers, professional soldiers and Hell's Angel-style bikers. Now they're on everyone from your favourite model to members of the Royal Family. They no longer ruin a serious career or any chances of modelling. Look at Sophie Anderton – she's got that long chain thing going right down her spine, while Katie Price and Nicole Ritchie have about 20 tattoos between them! Personally, I love them on men, and the more Tommy Lee they are the better. (Think Beckham if Tommy's not up your street.) But on girls I'm still undecided.

Having said for years that I would never get one, I've since changed my tune. Girls can have *a* tattoo, but more than one is tacky. Mine is a small black outline of a bow on my right hip. When asked, I always rather kinkily reply that it represents me as a 'gift' to anyone who sees it.

The truth is that I just really like bows. Maybe that's really gay, but when I was younger I used to buy pieces of ribbon and

48

lace from the local fabric shop and get my mum to tie them into a bow for me. I had bows everywhere! Once tattoos came into fashion, I saw a few like Jordan's pink bow on the base of her spine, and knew that if I ever got one that's what it would be.

I think classic tattoos, small and simple in black ink (not colour), look great on girls if they really mean something and they don't have too many. There's nothing worse than seeing a messy body. Have you ever seen Drew Barrymore in a bikini? I think she's great but jeez, she has tattoos dotted randomly about her body like she hasn't thought how they'll look all together. Because I have one on my right hip, I know I can't get any more on the front trunk of my body, or on my back now. (I already have a tattoo on the right-hand side of my body and I don't want to be uneven.)

You could purportedly even have three-month tattoos done at some of London's biggest and best-respected department stores, which seemed like the perfect solution if you were not 100 percent sure about what you wanted. But, shortly after hearing about it, I went to Selfridges and asked for this semi-permanent tattoo. It turned out to be a total urban myth!

I was still a little drunk from the night before, so my friend Kayla and I decided to just go ahead and get a real one. And so I am now a twice-tattooed lady, thus breaking my own one-tattoo rule. In case you're wondering, it's a swirly, italic version of my initials, FA, on the underside of my wrist. It was inspired by the VIP stamp you get at Paper, a great club on Regent Street. I love that stamp! Every Saturday morning I use to wake up and think, "Wow, that would look great as a tattoo!" Well, that morning I went and did it! (Got FA on my wrist, not a replica of the Paper stamp – that *would* be crazy! I love Paper, but not *that* much!)

Maybe we shouldn't think about tattoos too much, and they should symbolise only reckless abandon. Recently I went to Amsterdam with my best friends to celebrate a birthday – we had the best time ever, visiting a hilarious sex show and buying dodgy p*rn for my friend's boyfriend, when at some point I saw a tattoo shop with a dicey-looking guy brandishing a needle in the window. I was all down for getting a tattoo there and then, as I was having such a great time, but I was stopped before I ended up with something like 'Anne Frank Rocks My World' across my back. (Although it probably would have read, "ik houd van Anna Frank!")

It's not only you that you need to think about when getting inked; you need to think about future boyfriends and prospective husbands too. I've heard countless stories about men who can't date a girl with garish tattoos that are in your face, but I've never heard of a man refusing to date a girl with pure virgin skin. (I also heard that, to somebody who loves tattoos, nothing is more precious than bare, untouched flesh.)

Once upon a time I dated a guy who I shall call, for the purposes of this book, 'the Kuwaiti'. He was born into an important Arab family who dealt in oil and suchlike. So he was very well to do, but also something of a bore – scrap that, he was a *major* bore and a complete psycho to boot! However, when he mentioned the luxurious trips he took to his homeland I was tempted into going along.

But then he told me I wouldn't be able to wear a bikini out there, especially in front of his family. I demanded to know why! Not only was it my two best buddies (my implants) which were going to cause a problem, but apparently my tiny, pretty, non-offensive tattoo meant, in Kuwaiti terms, that I was a hooker. I'm still not 100 percent sure that it *does* mean that in Kuwait, but even so, his family would not have been impressed and I would have been warned off of their son.

Luckily for me, the Kuwaiti was a jackass anyway so it was no great loss. But let this be a valuable lesson to all you would-be inkers.

So in conclusion, yes, tattoos can lend you real character, and if there's a story behind them it's all good. Just make sure you don't end up with something hideous that you'll regret later, Amy Winehouse-stylee.

One of the worst tattoos I've seen on friends or family was on my ex-boyfriend, after he came back from holiday with his new girlfriend (she was icky by the way) with a huge, cartoon-style musical note on his shoulder. It came with the cheesy slogan, 'Music Is My Life' or something. What it really should have said is, "Accounts are my life – but I sometimes play the guitar (badly) at weekends."

Healthy, Wealthy and Wise ...

Being a party girl about town is hard on your mind, body, and sometimes even your soul. Take care of yourself as best you can when you're not downing vodka at an alarming rate, and hopefully you'll survive into your thirties relatively intact.

Living and working in central London, I end up eating out a lot. If I'm dating a guy, seeing a friend or even meeting up with my agent, it will invariably revolve around food. I also live right in the centre of Camden Town, which has a ridiculous amount of 24-hour fast-food restaurants to cater for all the weed-lovers with chronic munchies. It's lethal to someone looking to maintain a lower weight!

On the rare occasions that I feel like I should cook at home, my dinners are usually made by two very special men with extraordinary culinary talents: Uncle Ben and Captain Birdseye.

To make up for my appalling dietary habits, I try to be as healthy as I can during the day. I often find with healthy eating, or anything similarly tedious, that it's best to incorporate it into a daily routine and stick to it. I integrate mine into my working life, making sure I get into the office early to have a bowl of cereal to start the day. Every single afternoon I make myself a bowl of apple slices, strawberries, grapes, pineapple chunks or berries at a point that my co-worker calls, 'fruity time'. To make sure I'm getting all my nutrients I aim to drink six glasses of water a day. Sometimes I take a supplement if I'm feeling a little lacking in something (often iron, as I'm slightly anaemic). All this makes me feel much less guilty about all my vices.

So remember: eat right, exercise regularly – die anyway.

WAG Don't-Wannabe

Some Like it Haute

"I need something for my friend. Something that says:
'I'm not a slut, but I'm not a virgin either.'"
– White Chicks (2004 movie)

You may have noticed when you go to clubs in London, or any big city, that the girls' clothes are more outrageous, shorter, lower-cut and sparklier, and their heels are higher than what you would see back home. (If you come from a small town like I do, that is. Do keep up!) Read the party pages in *OK* if you're going for full-on glamour and the society pages in *Tatler* if you're going for the ruffled-up street urchin look. (I love *Tatler*, but what *is* it with these society girls who have to go out looking like they don't own a hairbrush, and the boys who look like they're a full-time surfer when the closest they ever got was probably a boogie board in Newquay?) Check out *London Lite*'s 'London Eye' pages to see what people are wearing at the clubs you're going to, as it can spark creativity and inspiration in your own dress style.

Don't be afraid of what you're spending. If I love a Chloe bag for £2000 and I can afford it, then I will buy it, because no one else on the high street can capture the great design and baby-soft leather of Chloe. But if I see a great pair of shoes in Primark for £6 then I will buy those too. I'm not worried that people will look at something I'm wearing and know it's from Primark or New Look – in fact I'm more willing to reveal the cost of a bargain in TK Maxx than a splurge in Selfridges. Mixing cheaper-than-chips and designer bits is the art of intelligent shopping. When I was younger all I could afford, and all I wanted to buy, were high-street copies. Now I've matured a bit, I understand the value of such things as good shoes.

> *"My feet are still on the ground, I'm just wearing better shoes."* – Oprah Winfrey

Shoes are the thing that I am most ready to loosen the tight grip on my purse for. I'm prepared to splash out £400 on Louboutin and Gina heels, as they're made so well, but, at the same time, if I see fun leopard print and patent winkle-pickers for sale in New Look at £20 I will snap them up with just as much enthusiasm! Gina shoes are the holy grail. They sparkle like nothing else on earth, and will make your legs look longer and slimmer than you thought possible! One place you should definitely visit for its foot candy is the Shoe Boudoir in Harrods at Knightsbridge. If you get something in black or gold/silver/diamonds then you can wear them with everything. It's money well spent.

The internet is a great place to find unusual party-wear. Check out Leg Avenue's stuff – some of the dresses are very daring, but totally worth it! I got a little black lace number from there once, with a v-neck that almost came down to my belly button, and it definitely had the desired effect (bar a few pervs). Log onto eBay and find seller's shops that specialise in party wear. Type in things like, 'sexy dress', 'party dress' or 'gorgeous couture', and it will come up with a whole host of things. You'll triple your scope if you look on the US version of eBay; as the pound is generally stronger than the dollar you can pick up some real bargains. As they say, one man's trash is another man's treasure.

Don't dismiss your local market. There are some great ones all over the country; out in Essex there's the infamous Dagenham Market, and Pitsea, which is good on a Saturday. Camden High Street is amazing for party dresses. There's one little shop where you can take in a page of a magazine and they will base a dress on it for you! Luckily, I live right on the high street and at the centre of the markets, so it's all on my doorstep. (I check them out every couple of days or so as their turnover is so high.)

Although I love a good market, some of the things you see may err on the wrong side of dodgy – a bit too bling, a bit too chavvy. But once you take them out of the setting of Dagenham Dave's stall and into the bar at the Sanderson, mixing them with your designer shoes and classy handbag, they can easily be transformed.

Use your imagination to put together great combos – they don't need to be designer outfits, as smart girls spend wisely. Save that for when you have a footballer's wage to burn. Besides which, as we've noted before, footballers are really simple creatures. If you really do want to ensure their attention, then dress accordingly. Make skirts that little bit shorter, necklines that little bit lower, heels that little bit higher. Footballers are essentially just chavs with cash. If there's one thing I've learned from watching them and guys of similar financial status, it's that you must never confuse money with class. They really are two separate things.

It's true, there are a certain class of men that like that whole 'tits and ass' style. (And I am a mistress of just such a style!) Whilst some may lust after page three models in *The Sun*, men who are slightly more mature, cultured and – dare I say it, at the risk of sounding like a fascist? – educated may feel the same about the Pirelli calendar, which is a lot more arty but by no means less sexy. I guess what I'm trying to say is that, as a smart girl, you need to know your market. If you're in the market for a footballer this week, then dress accordingly. When you decide to move on to more substantial, long-term relationships then change to suit.

Before any angry, hairy-legged feminists start protesting, it's not about changing *you* – it's about *clothes*!

WOULD LIKE TO MEET

"Nights are not just for sleep." – Marilyn Monroe

Go to the best clubs. Don't stand with the masses, get in VIP. Call up the club beforehand and wangle your way in. Get to know one of the door staff, or contact a party promoter. Footballers do not often sit in the main area of the club, unless it's a really exclusive one.

Footballers are fun to have a fling with, to mess around with. They're a thrill, a shot of adrenaline. They're a bit like going on that absolutely terrifying ride at Alton Towers – Oblivion I think it's called – where you're suspended above a huge black hole and go plummeting head-first in. The only difference here is that it lasts slightly longer.

But you wouldn't want to spend your whole life on Oblivion, would you? To live in constant fear and be plunged into darkness on a regular basis? Likewise, you don't want to marry somebody terribly boring, like an accountant from Slough (the equivalent of the Tea Cups ride). You're looking for something in between – but as a party girl about town you're nowhere near thinking about marriage yet – and so, for now, Oblivion it is! (Just ensure you know what ride you're on before you get strapped in.) But so many girls don't have the first clue about how to meet footballers, or any eligible men for that matter.[*]

Footballers are renowned for being money-rich, taste-poor. You're not going to be seeing them puffing on a cigar in Aspinall's or lunching in Soho House, and they wouldn't recognise the charm of a Mark Birley club if it hit them in the face. You're far more likely to see them burning £50 notes (yes, this does happen), pouring Cristal down z-list models' silicone valleys (classy!) or vomiting all over themselves before being carried out by security at the Embassy or Faces in Essex.

So pick your city. Up north, in places like Newcastle, the teams and players are treated like gods, and their VIP sections are more secure than Steven Gerrard's house, post-gangster-attack. It's imperative that you know somebody in order to get in the right club on the right night.

If you're going on a weekend away to a new city find out the best places to go via acquaintances who live or work in that area, promoters, or the more mechanical method of Facebook or Myspace. (More of that later.) The top cities in

---

[*] But please do not mistake a footballer for an eligible man. An eligible man, by definition, is boyfriend, if not husband, material. A footballer is neither of these things.

which to find hot ballers include Liverpool, Manchester, Newcastle and, of course, London.

Clubs often aren't ashamed to boast that the local team frequent their club – so check it out! Now start on your research. First of all, check that the team from the city you're going to:

Doesn't have an away game that weekend. (In which case they simply won't be there, except maybe for some skanky reserves who didn't even make the bench.)

Doesn't have a game on Sunday. (They won't be allowed out Saturday night – by strict orders.)

Has a home game – if they win the whole team will be out celebrating, and where there are celebrations there's lots of scandal to be had!

No good explorer would wander off into the jungle without conducting some much-needed research, and so neither should you. Whilst in your jungle, you may not be mauled by a lion or poisoned by an exotic plant, but you could very well be attacked by a clipboard-wielding door-Nazi, or lured into a roasting session before you can say 'Aunt Bessie's Yorkshire Puddings'.

Log on to the club's official page and check out Player Profiles – these have pictures of each player, their names, and boring football statistics like how many goals they've scored, their inside leg measurement or something equally tedious. (Why don't they change them to something more useful or interesting, like 'weekly wage' and 'girth measurement when erect'?)

They also rather peculiarly state whether they are right- or left-footed. Last time I checked, I was more or less ambidextrous with my feet. If one foot happened to take more steps than the other, then surely we would all be walking around in circles? But I've just been informed by the trusty old internet that this refers to which foot they prefer to kick the damned ball with – which I think speaks volumes as to how terribly silly these 'facts' are. Still, the profiles are handy to print out so you can swot up on the way there and recognise some of the faces.

> *"Despite its drawbacks, that's the beauty of the London party scene. With all its sleaze, drugs and superficiality, a random encounter with a unique person is always a possibility and that's what made the scene so alluring to me."* – Cassie Sumner

I've been a regular on London's infamous party circuit for about two years now. So many times you'll catch the eye of some guy who looks familiar, but you just can't place him. Maybe you had a not-very-memorable date with him once, or you just saw him on the tube. But the fact is, if you're going to the clubs and places I suggest then it's probably a footballer you've glanced at on *Match of the Day* (although I don't know why you'd be watching this), or in the back pages of your favourite red top.

The fact that I met Wesley and a number of other guys totally by chance (and certainly didn't recognise *him*!) makes me realise that a ton of famous footballers have just passed me by. If it had been my aim (as it is with a lot of girls) to actively find one, then via conducting some vital research the opportunities would have been tenfold!

I remember once, when I was having the best steak of my life at Shoreditch House, that I was sat next to some guy all night who's apparently huge in the British music industry. Even now I can't quite place his name, but he's some kind of indie/rock musician. Much to the dismay of the Sony music producer I was dining with, I was totally oblivious all night. He only told me when we were walking (quickly, looking over our shoulders – after all, we were in east London) to the car, and quite rightly I was livid. Had he informed me (discreetly of course) beforehand, I could have endeared myself to 'Indie Guy' and the possibility of being invited to all manner of glamorous occasions would have opened up before me. I'm sure he would have been glad of the company, as he was with a rather miserable, scruffy-looking man and they were barely uttering a thing to one another.

But if any players particularly stand out as hotties, Google them individually. A good site to check is Wikipedia, as it has a Personal Details section which will tell you if they're married, single or have children. Knowledge is power, girls, and it's good to know what you're up against – but knowledge is useless without the conviction to use it.*

Knowing the marital/personal situation of somebody you

---

* *Please don't think me a terrible stalker for knowing all of this – I only chanced upon my research methods when trying to find out more about my mysterious beau, 'Wesley'. With hindsight they're terribly good tactics though.*

wish to date/have sexytime with is vital. Although I know just how easy it would be for a girl using this guide to start seeing a footballer, you must remember that I didn't employ these tactics for myself, but stumbled upon them during my travels. When I met Wesley I had no idea he had a long-term girlfriend and young child, otherwise there's no way I would have gone there. Having found out over a month into our 'affair', I was already very emotionally involved.

I hope that will explain my poor judgement in deciding to continue. I do not criticise people who have affairs with married people, as some feelings are too strong to overcome, and, as I've said before, it's the married parties' relationship to protect – not yours or mine. Despite my views that girls like Aimee Walton and Rebecca Loos have done wives-in-the-dark/doormats like Cheryl Cole and Victoria Beckham a huge favour, purposely targeting a married man is not something I would advise either morally or emotionally.

London – Not Just a City, but a State of Mind

Wayne: *"Here we are at Piccadilly Circus!"*
Garth: *"What a shitty circus."*
Wayne: *"Good call, there's no clowns or animals …*
What a rip-off!" – *Wayne's World 2*

A wise man once said that when you're tired of London, you're tired of life. I couldn't agree more. I love this city and can't understand some of my friends from back home, or my strange sister, who hate it and want to stay in quiet suburbs with one pub and an Indian takeaway. Not only is London superb for culture and entertainment, it just so happens that it's the ultimate place for footballers.

Up north it's just too crazy and hyped. Northerners don't really have too many other celebrities than footballers, besides perhaps the casts of *Hollyoaks and Coronation Street*. Whereas footballers can easily go out clubbing in London without being noticed. There are simply far too many music stars, It girls, socialites, models, party girls and playboys going about their business.

Just the other night I was at Chinawhite when Trashy – sorry, Ashley – Cole was there with a couple of team-mates. Contrary to wildly speculative reports in the papers the next day, they went largely unnoticed once inside.

Not only that, there are so many football clubs to choose from! Arsenal, West Ham, Tottenham, Chelsea, plus lower-league lovelies like Queens Park Rangers to make up the numbers. Say there are 20 players per team[*] – that's over 100 Premiership footballers at your disposal. Okay, so a small percentage might be gay, an even smaller percentage might be in totally monogamous relationships, but there are still plenty who are ripe for the picking!

First things first though. Remember the rules. Before going out, check if there's a match the next day, in which case the team aren't out playing that night. Secondly, swot up on

---

[*] *I'm totally guessing the number. Researching actual football isn't a great hobby of mine. Let your dad patronisingly correct me.*

faces – even if you don't remember the names, it doesn't matter. You will have to lie and pretend you don't know them anyway. (More about that later.)

Secondly, no girl in her right mind would just go to a club on her own. And I don't just mean with no friends (that's plain crazy), I mean without inside support. There are hundreds of promoters in London – use them, and use them wisely! They're paid to bring hot party girls into all the top clubs, and you in return get to instantly jump the queue, plus free entry, free drinks all night, and – most importantly – access to a top table, often in the VIP section of the club.

Party, Party, Party!

> *"I get here and Mr Harper here makes me feel like*
> *I'm some dumb blonde with fake boobs going to a*
> *Hugh Hefner party."* – Tiffany Wilson, *White Chicks*
> *"Alcohol – the cause of, and solution to, all of*
> *life's problems."* – Homer Simpson

Promoters, like different vodkas, can be a major factor of a great night out or else just leave a bad taste in your mouth. So check them out and give them a chance. Most have Myspace or Facebook pages. Good ones will have lots of girls as friends, and a ton of pictures of their nights out. Check out the pictures and look out for the particular parties they went to.

Were they invited to big events you remember, like the

WAG Don't-Wannabe

P Diddy party when he was in London last? Are their tables full of hot girls or just coked-up slags? Are any of their friends celebrities/nonebrities, models or footballers? Are there any footballers in their pictures, or any other celebrities/nonebrities?

(Calum Best and Adee Phelan's gang don't count – they are table-whores who rock up to the clubs every night of the week!)

Remember, hardly any footballers go on a night out without a party organiser. It will do you good to get in with these guys and party regularly with them – so that when a footballer has a big night out, you'll be one of the first people he will call to make it *one to remember!*

Just in case you're new to this, I don't mean that in a hooker-ish way – I mean that he will ensure everyone (including you and other hot girls) gets plenty to drink and anything else you want. What you do afterwards is totally up to you – whether it's bedding a player you really like at a hotel after-party (I would not advise this – see 'After-Parties' section!) or visiting a 24-hour McDonald's on the way home and Facebooking in your pj's at 5:00am. Again, it's all up to you!

Promoters all get different deals with different clubs. Look out for what they're drinking in the pictures. If you're not a big champagne buff, then look for the vodka. Sputnik,[*] or even worse, Absolut, are no-goes on the big tables. Look out

---

[*] *Apparently some people really like Sputnik and say it's a good vodka. I beg to disagree. If we sampled vodkas like wine tasters, swilling it around our mouths, I would choke on the fumes before you could say "triple distilled".*

for Belvedere, Snow Queen, and the firm favourite of London footballers (and *moi*), Grey Goose.

Promoters also get different tables; each club has different ranking tables, decided by how much you must spend on each. (Well, not *you* personally, of course!) For example, on a Wednesday night in Chinawhite the best table is number four, which is on the raised platform at the back. In Amika it's the 'Owner's Table', which is the only secluded table in the Champagne Lounge. Princess Beatrice and Kanye West have both had the privilege of that table, as well as yours truly on many occasions.

Francesca's Survival Rules for Party Girls

> *"The key to a good party is having someone else pay for it."* – Perez Hilton

Get to know who are the good promoters and which are the bad. Bad promoters force you to drink or, worse, have too little drink to go around, stage crap nights at even crappier clubs and pressurise you. Good promoters are like friends and you must be loyal to them. It's perfectly acceptable to have more than one promoter friend if they do different nights at different clubs, but don't dart about.

Always text or email a promoter any names you want him to put on the guest list by, at the latest, 5:00pm that day. It's not fair to spring names on them later on, as they have to send off their lists to the club by a certain time.

I used to date a promoter for about six months, and every night I saw him we would be constantly interrupted by girls calling and texting, asking to go on one guest list or another. It really wasn't fair (particularly on me), as it always used to happen at the worst possible moment, if you know what I mean. (Wink wink!) It makes for a very stressful night, and being the cause of someone's stress is neither nice nor funny. (Unless you are doing it purely to annoy someone, which is different.)

Promoters get a tough time about which girls they bring to the club, as they're supposed to be hotter than hot. There's no such thing as a free lunch – or free vodka in this case – and, although you're getting your nights out paid for, you should repay it by being reliably well-turned out in appropriate dress, nice shoes, a rocking tan and well-groomed hair. This isn't your local dive and you're not Peaches Geldof – you can't expect to turn up looking like Beth Ditto, or Britney Spears after her breakdown, and expect to get VIP treatment.

Know the dress code and stick with it. Some clubs are much dressier than others and little party frocks do the job perfectly. Other nights, such as Paper on a Friday, you can get away with a teeny pair of shorts or, on rare occasions, jeans instead.

Don't abuse the alcohol. It's generally good etiquette to wait for the waitress (if on a private table) or the promoter (if on a party table) to pour the drinks. You're not the only one there and there are others to consider. Some girls do try to hog the vodka bottle, but it's rather vulgar. (If you do happen to see them at the end of the night, you'll probably find them catching the night bus back to some hole in Zone Five, if not farther.)

Don't get too wasted. I really should practice what I preach here, as I am well known for getting drunk beyond belief. But those who make the mistakes learn the lessons best! There's fun/flirty/dancey drunk and then there's crazy, lurching-around drunk. You do not wish to be the latter.

Don't do drugs. I know it's obvious that half of London's club revellers are on coke, but that doesn't mean *you* need to be. It's really unbecoming of young ladies to be doing this (as my mother often tells me). It wastes your looks, time, money and anything else you have to lose – including your job and your dignity at some point. You may think having a quick line in the toilet isn't that bad, but you're just one dicey step away from becoming a crackhead *a la* Miss Winehouse. WAG don't-wannabes want a life *after* the partying. But if you dabble too much you may as well kiss your life goodbye and start hanging around with Pete Doherty.

Make friends. Yes, other girls can be really bitchy and jealous, and you could cut the air around some clubs with a Gina stiletto. But others are perfectly nice, just like you! It's worth befriending some of them as you will probably see them around a lot. One day, you might want to go to a party with one of them when your usual party buddies are busy. So always smile, be polite and, if you're going to bitch, don't do it too loudly. If you've been drinking, you're probably talking a lot louder than you realise!

I remember once I was at a club back in Essex, with a good

friend of mine called Jen. We bumped into two girls we went to school with, and politely (so I thought) stopped to talk to them. I was drunk so, after I'd been asking one of the girls about her baby, I turned to Jen and said (discreetly, so I thought, but she later informed me I was very loud), "I hate that girl! I really, really hate her! Let's go!" The two girls heard every blatant word as I was shouting it out about half a metre away from their ears. The strange thing is, I didn't really hate her. Oh well. I moved to London about a fortnight later, so I've not seen them since.

Be courteous. No matter how many drunken louts and chavs you're surrounded by, never leave your manners at the door. At the end of the night remember to thank your promoter and say goodbye. Sometimes, if you forget or can't find him, you can send him an email or a text the next day to say thank you. Don't do a Cheryl Cole – always be polite, thanking toilet attendants and door staff. You may be in a dress that's shorter than your actual underwear and half off of your face, but you were still well brought up. People remember your manners a lot more than they remember what you were wearing.

After-Parties

"The after party's at my body" – Jennifer Lopez

After-parties are the norm and, while you don't want to seem a total party-pooper prude by not going along, be careful.

They're usually held in a suite of a hotel, somewhere like the Lanesborough, the Westbury or the Mayfair Hotel. Alternatively, if someone in the group has a huge house in the centre of town it can be held there.

One guy I knew had a permanent suite at the Lanesborough. If you're in London you have to go there. It's a beautiful old building at Hyde Park Corner that used to be a hospital. Now it's a St Regis hotel. When you go inside it's like stepping back in time. The rooms are all high ceilings, dark wood panelling, period features and wall canvasses. It's amazing.

Back then, loads of us would always go back afterwards for some good room-service food and a movie in bed. The amount of people that used to get in that bed at one time was crazy! But it was always really fun and I felt safe there. However, things can take a more sinister turn.

Back in my more naïve days, when I first started going out in London, I was invited to a party at Mo*vida with my friend, who was a glamour model. This is one of my all-time favourite clubs and we had a great time with a bunch of guys that our promoter, Carlton, knew. They were all over from Dubai, where they were billionaire oil sheikhs, coming to London once a month for a few days of mayhem. When they suggested an after-party at a hotel they were staying in, Carlton seemed to know them well enough so we agreed to go along. We all got into chauffeured cars that were waiting outside for a 30-second drive to the Westbury Hotel. The guys had a huge suite and by the time we rocked up there was already some kind of party going on.

WAG Don't-Wannabe

In the main living area a couple of lithe naked girls were walking around, snorting coke, mostly off of other naked girls' bodies. Guys (who were fully clothed) were knocking back drinks and encouraging the girls to do things with each other that I daren't write, for fear of tainting this book forever. I should have got out then, but I didn't.

Some girls who were at our table back at the club were leaving as we arrived, and begged me to go with them. I dismissed them as crazy, or coked-up. Besides, although I am totally against hard drugs, I'm quite liberal. This was only a bit of nakedness and stuff – I was sure that far worse happened at the Playboy Mansion!

So I sat down with Carlton, my friend, and a couple of the guys we were with. They offered me a drink – vodka and something, I couldn't really tell. I drank it, and that's more or less the last thing I can be 100 percent sure of remembering correctly. Although my mind wasn't totally gone, I remember being aware that I couldn't move my body. Before I knew it I was laying on a bed, not feeling very well at all.

I kept slipping in and out of consciousness. When I woke up there were a lot more people on the bed, some engaged in sexual activities. I do remember *not* wanting to see any of that!

I woke up more than once with two particular guys alternately sitting on me, holding my arms down. They needn't have bothered; I couldn't have lifted them if I tried. I liken the feeling to when you come around from anaesthetic. In your mind you're there, but when you try to speak or move you just can't. Those two guys wouldn't leave me alone, although I'm pretty damned sure they didn't do anything to me apart from somehow getting some of my clothes off.

One man, who I shall call K, had to come in more than once to get them off of me after I regained my power of speech and shouted for him. He ended up staying with me most of the night to keep them away, and for that I will always be grateful. I slept and slept and slept until whatever I had been given had worn off. When I woke up in the morning we laid and talked for hours.

There were strange girls and random Arabs dotted about the floor in various states of undress and unconsciousness. It was hardly the most romantic setting, but I think I fell for K then, just a little bit. I thanked him again and again for practically saving my life the night before, and he asked to see me again that night. At the time I lived all the way out in Essex, and the fact that it was already 2pm – along with the less-than-relaxing night before – meant that the chances of me coming back for more were slim to none.

I had nothing with me except a tiny bag. The dress I'd been wearing the night before was nowhere to be seen. He offered to take me shopping at Harrods and buy me some new clothes to wear, even makeup and straighteners. It's not really my style to accept, so I didn't. Instead, I made full use of the hotel concierge by getting him to fetch me a toothbrush and other necessities, and tried to make myself as presentable as possible. With as much dignity as I could muster, I rode the lift down to the lobby of a five-star hotel on a Saturday lunchtime, in a slightly see-through short dress and high heels. And so I began my walk of shame, which luckily lasted only a few steps outside the lobby and into a chauffeur-driven Mercedes that was to take me all the way home, courtesy of kind, sweet K.

I met those girls who urged me to leave with them just a few months ago, over a year after the incident. They were in a club in Kensington and recognised me immediately. I told them what had happened, and all of the things I had seen at that party, and they said they felt guilty for letting me go in there. I'm glad I did though. No one learns a lesson better than she who makes a mistake. I know now to be more wary of my surroundings and any drinks that are offered. Luckily, nothing really bad happened to me that night. It could have been a lot worse.

The worst thing to come out of this was that, after an argument some months later that occurred, rather randomly, in the middle of Africa (the continent, not some hip new club!), Carlton told anyone who would listen that I was part of some crazy, drug-fuelled orgy that night. The things that he said I did are things I've never even *seen* anyone do! At least K and I knew the truth. And besides, Carlton left the party soon after leaving me in the clutches of people I barely knew, and certainly couldn't trust.

That experience definitely made me more wary of the people I hung around with at parties, but it didn't curb my insatiable appetite for clubs, alcohol and everything that comes with them.

My Top Tips for After-Parties

- Only go with friends and people you know and trust. If you don't know the main group of people then take at least two friends with you – and don't get separated.
- Watch every drink that's made for you and never leave it lying around. There is a chance that the whole bottle of vodka is laced, so you won't actually see any tampering. In this case, try to drink from bottles that you've seen being opened. Or don't drink at all.
- Lots of after-parties get naked – with huge hotel bathtubs, round revolving beds and showers taking centre stage. Only join in if you feel comfortable with the people you're with. Some (Neanderthal) men see your involvement in a naked party as an open invitation to copulation, so the best way to join in the fun whilst keeping your distance is to strip down, but keep any underwear (sans yours top, obviously) firmly on.
- Trust your instincts, not what people tell you. Your instincts have amazing accuracy and the more you use them the more they work. If something doesn't feel right it probably isn't. Get out of the situation.
- *"I'm not worried because there is no tape ... there is* no *tape!"* – Abi Titmuss. Even though it may seem a really good idea at the time to 'do a Paris' and make your own movie with a videophone – don't! This can only end in tears – just look at poor Abi. Likewise, don't let anyone else film you either, and be aware of voyeurs who may be

filming out of wardrobes or from the floor. You don't want to find yourself the next star of YouTube.

Football Clubs' Christmas Parties – a.k.a. the Meat Market, including Full Roast

By the time Christmas 2007 rolled around, I had been seeing Wesley for almost seven months. We'd had our highs and lows and had just been through our toughest time yet. Just weeks previously, my friend who had so often lent us her flat had sold her story to the *News of the World*, and Wesley had found out. I was virtually held hostage in his solicitors' offices for over nine hours, but we eventually came to some kind of agreement.

All was forgiven, but things were strained. I had found out that he and his girlfriend had temporarily separated, and we hadn't seen each other in 'that way' since. He had offered me the world, literally – a chance to go anywhere for as long as I liked with as many of my friends as I chose. To the annoyance of my friends, I turned everything down. I wanted to prove that I didn't want anything from him, as I'd never taken anything before. Emotions were high and my heart was fragile. Going to his Christmas party was the worst thing I could have done ...

Come Christmastime, you will get invited to all the football clubs' official parties. Reader beware! Although you can pretty much guarantee every player will be there, in high spirits and having a good time, it's not all it's cracked up to be. If you can resist, stay well away!

Last Christmas I went to the party for the top London club that Wesley plays for, held in a trendy club I love in west London. The party organiser who gave Wesley my phone number when I very first met him had invited me. I couldn't wait to go, and got a friend to come along. What a shocker I was in for!

The club had paid party organisers to fill the entire place with scantily clad girls. Not a single man in sight, except for maybe two or three who were running things. It was the oddest thing ever – I felt like I was in a lesbian's dream.

20 guys and 200 girls – you do the maths. As I looked around the room I noticed the eager, somewhat desperate gazes of these young girls (though some were old enough to know better). They craned their necks, seeking out the golden ticket – a footballer! Their ticket to stardom and endless shopping sprees, or maybe a perfume deal, a newspaper column or fashion line. Failing that, a roasting in the toilets and a kiss-and-tell the following week would do.

The football team, including Wesley, eventually turned up at around eleven after drinking in a well-known casino for the last few hours. (A few too many hours by the look of things.) We went and drank and danced in the VIP area with the team, but shy girls beware – there is no room for shrinking violets here! Be prepared to face hostility from other girls as they fight to sit next to the most desirable players. Everyone, not just the players, is out for themselves.

We got talking to a couple of girls who told me how they had already been to another big London club's party that year, and that one of them had a one-night stand with one of the players. She was clear that her mission tonight was to get the same result. Although I totally understand (probably better than a lot of people) why she would want to do that, it's a very different story when someone into whom you've invested months of time and affection becomes the target of someone like her. I suddenly wanted Wesley to really be called 'Wesley'. For him to be just an ordinary guy, a personal trainer, and for us not to have to be there with all those people. But of course, it wouldn't be the same then, would it?

As hard as I tried to have a good time, I couldn't. Instead I drank … and drank … and drank. Wesley came on hot, then cold, then hot again. I was freaked out. Everything about our relationship had always been so secretive, then suddenly here we were in public and we still had to be so careful about showing affection. I just wanted to kiss him and, soon enough, I did anyway. The night passed in a blur of intense passion one minute and screaming, jealous hatred the next. You may be surprised to hear that the jealousy wasn't mine (at least not outwardly) but his.

So while he was off drunkenly talking to people (he's well-known for being a total lightweight, bless him), I thought I would play the age-old trick – making someone jealous just by talking to someone else. I got chatting to a boy who was sweeter than icing sugar. He was younger than me and looked too pure and innocent to be there. Totally down to earth, he was nothing like most of the other prima donna team-mates around him. I did something which I had completely forgotten about until I came to write it now – almost six months later. (That's alcohol abuse for you.) I told him all about Wesley and I.

I figured half of them probably knew anyway, from how we had been acting. Wesley was always kind, understanding and sympathetic. I sometimes see him in the back pages of the tabloids now and he seems to be doing really well, playing for the first team a lot and even scoring some goals. I hope he stays just as sweet as he was.

After the young player and I had been talking and dancing together for a while, Wesley asked me to go and sit down with him over the other side of the room. It was quiet over there, less crowded, so we would have more of a chance to talk (at least as much as the joint consumption of a whole bottle of Grey Goose would allow).

Then he went crazy, asking me why I'd been talking to his team-mate, what were we talking about, did I like the kid? Whoa, I wasn't prepared for that! Wesley is tall, dark and – well, not a lot of people regard him as handsome, but I thought he was. And the boy I was talking to was just that. A boy. Short, pasty and ginger. Not my type at all. But Wesley's jealously was a new one on me and I was rather enjoying his discomfort!

Wesley explained that his girlfriend's brother was at the party but he wanted to take me home, pretty soon in fact. I wasn't going to argue. The atmosphere in the club that night was so horrible that I still sometimes have nightmares about it. Melodramatic but true. Have a relationship with someone for over half a year, then go to a party where every girl wants to pull him, drink half a bottle of vodka each and get him to act like a twat, then see how *you* feel. You'd freak out too.

The night ended with me deciding to go home. It was late, and the car to take my friend and I back to Essex was waiting. Ever polite, I told Wesley I was leaving and that I would text him in the morning. I expected him to be fine, but he told me to wait as he was coming with me. I was surprised but nonetheless, like the damned *fool* that I am, I waited. When Wesley eventually came he was all over the place, trying to kiss me, then saying he couldn't leave with me as he would be seen. I'd now been waiting over half an hour and my poor friend, who had rather overindulged, was sick, narrowly missing my Ginas. Not only that but it was a weeknight, and I had to be up for work in less than four hours.

I wanted to go home.

After another ten minutes of fannying around I told Wesley I was leaving and walked out, only for him to grab me and try to pull me back. At this point about three or four of his friends got involved, holding him back and ushering him into a car that was waiting outside. I was seriously pissed now, as I'd been waiting for him to get his act together for too long. I could have been on the A13, having a little nap, not standing outside a club, watching him behave like a rather large, drunken child. In the end I decided to simply kick the car he had gotten into – which bloody hurt – and go home.

You would think that was the end. But no. Just as we set off he kept calling and telling me that his friends had bundled him in there against his will, and that he wanted our car to follow his so we could meet up. Our rather pissed-off taxi driver was having none of it. He wanted to get back to Essex, never mind the fact that I was paying him, the cheeky freaking idiot. So I just turned off my phone and tried to forget about the whole messy night and grab a few minutes' sleep.

No such luck. I'm fortunate that I have such fun-loving party pals who throw themselves whole-heartedly into any cocktail that's put in front of them, but it backfired just then. My friend was having a serious regurgitation moment, and had to scream at the driver to stop on the hard shoulder for her to be sick.

And so, halfway down the A13, in somewhere 'proper rough' like Canning Town, rubbing a vomiting friend's back and exclaiming at what was coming out ("What in hell did you eat?! There's all kinds of crazy shit here! Now do you want me to take a picture, because you *will* thank me in the morning?!"), whilst trying to pacify an irate driver, I ended my first and last ever football club Christmas party. What a way to celebrate the birth of Jesus Christ.

Funnily enough, that little incident has become common-place for Wesley recently. I regularly see him in the papers, falling out of a club minus his clothing, his awareness of time and space or his dignity. He's always being thrown out for being unable to stand up, fighting with other customers, etc.

That makes me feel a bit better. For ages, I was beating myself up about how that night ended. It wasn't helped by the friend who accompanied me telling all and sundry about it. So thanks for that. It wasn't just once either – at every function, party, event, holiday or gathering, formal or otherwise, whenever there was a lull in conversation, the 'Fran and Wesley's row' story was wheeled out like a gimp for everyone's entertainment.

Wesley is a sore subject with me anyway – as you may have gathered. But, although I hate it happening to me, I do find it funny when others are subjected to the same treatment. Another one of my good friends, Sophia, often gets her story retold at every opportunity. (Of course, hers is funnier than mine, which is *not* amusing at all.)

We were in Ibiza last summer and became friends with a group of guys. One day we were all sitting around the pool, discussing tattoos. Sophia got up and exclaimed, "Look at this!" She meant to pull down her bikini bottoms a little to show a small tattoo of a red and orange flower, but she was drunk and pulled them down a bit far, basically showing the whole group her bouff. This happened over six months ago yet still gets brought up now, much to her annoyance (and my amusement).

But I digress again.

About a month after our row I found myself in the offices of *The People*, with Wesley's lawyers faxing over statements left, right and centre. This is when I saw that he had stooped to a new low. He said that, on that night, I had attacked and threatened him and that (get this!) he was "scared for his life". Now I'm sorry, but the guy is over six feet and I am a weakling girl.

Luckily, one of my saving graces that day was that I had saved all my text messages and had them photographed by the newspaper. I had texts on file from him an hour after that incident, begging me to go and meet him, to see him the very next day, telling me that he missed me.

Ha! He messed with the wrong blonde that day. All the proof was there on my little gold phone and his ridiculous claims were dismissed as pure fabrication. The story went ahead in *The People*, but I decided not to name him. I don't think I ever will ...

Perversely enough, I think that an organised footballers' party is the very worst place and situation in which to meet a footballer, despite it being the one time you can pretty much guarantee a whole team in one room. After all, my entire theory of how to bag yourself a baller is based on acting dumb and pretending to not know who they are. If you turn up along with a gaggle of other girls, each one more fake-tanned, fake-nailed, fake-haired and fake-boobed than the last, this is totally going to blow your cover.

Not only this, but when they meet girls at these free-for-alls they're going with one-night sex and infidelity solely in mind. I think that if I'd known who Wesley was I wouldn't have been able to act as cool as I did. (By cool, I don't mean in a Carlton from *Fresh Prince of Bel Air* way, but in the stand-offish, hard-to-get way that I am with almost every man I meet. It drives them wild.)

We also met in a more sophisticated environment without every gold-digging thrill-seeker in town turning up, which made it much easier for us to be equals in each other's eyes. This is very important for a balanced relationship. (As ours was in the beginning.) The fact that my boyfriend at the time had him forcibly removed from the club for talking to me gave me a little bit more authority than most girls he'd meet in a club. Not that I'm condoning my ex's behaviour – I hated it when he did that to guys for almost no reason – but I think it was this that made Wesley and I last much longer than a little one-night stand, as I appeared unobtainable to him.

Still, the Christmas party really opened my eyes to what the footballer's lifestyle is all about. For the first time ever, it genuinely made me thankful that I wasn't tied to one of them by marriage – or even worse, a child. Your body is never the same after a baby, so save it for someone who's worth it. Footballers invariably aren't.

My first chance encounter with a footballer came a couple of years ago, long before I even knew that someone could be right- or left-footed or this book began. It was my 21st birthday and my friends and I were headed for a weekend of fun in Newcastle. I have a good friend I met through my old job as a PA who we'll call Geordie. He met us in Newcastle and assured me that, if I was with him, I could go wherever I wanted, whenever I wanted – he would make it a birthday to remember! He also promised me footballers.

Hello? Just because I'm blonde, from Essex and have fake boobs doesn't mean I want to date a footballer! Well ... OK.

So before we went, we did a little research on the Newcastle United team – just to see what they looked like and if there were any hotties!

There were. It was really never my intention to meet one though, as it was totally *not* my style at that time. I had a steady boyfriend of two years and had enough of a stereotyped image without adding a footballer to the list.

Anyway, we end up in Tiger Tiger (don't judge me on that – the Newcastle one is *hot!*), it's really crowded and full of crazy people on hen and stag nights, so Geordie and I head off to the VIP lounge. We're not in there long when Geordie points out that there's a group of footballers he knows. I only recognise one, who played for England. (I wasn't that up on football at the time.) There was a really hot guy with them who looked a bit like Kelly Jones from Stereophonics – let's call him Paddy, as that was his name. He was really sweet and we chatted all night.

There were a load of other guys there – footballers, I assumed – and one tried to talk to me once or twice. Now let me tell you about what I've observed ever since then in the presence of footballers. Those girls that are out there just to bag one at any cost are *sick*. There we were, chatting away, and some of them were just literally doing anything to get their attention. The memory of one practically doing a lap dance to a table leg makes me shudder even now. It was like I'd suddenly found myself in a queue of crazy wannabes auditioning for *Big Brother*! I wasn't that fussed though – I didn't recognise any of those guys anyway.

During the course of the night I was asked back to their 'party'. Although the Absolut vodka-fuelled, gold-digger part of my brain was screaming YES, sense prevailed and I declined. I didn't really want to be handcuffed to a bed and filmed along with the desperate lap-dancing girl. (Well, that's what happens, isn't it?)

It's getting on for 3am and I'm so tired I have to go back to the hotel. I tell Paddy I have to leave and he suddenly pounces, asking for my number. *Jackpot!* I think. He's sweet, he's not a footballer (so I know he's not crazy) and he's dead hot! What more could you want? So I give it to him but here's where it starts to get weird. He says he'll text me in the morning but he'll have changed his number by then. Huh?

Little did I suspect it was to be the beginning of the weirdest 'relationship' I have ever had. Incredibly, a Premiership footballer had looked through the queue (I'm not exaggerating) of *Big Bro*-stylee contestant girls half-naked and in-your-face, with offers of things that I couldn't even imagine, and had singled out the Essex girl in the corner in a £3 Primark top, chatting to the only non-famous guy in the room. Don't you just *love* it when things work out like that?

As you can see from my experience, even though back then I was genuinely naïve, it's imperative to remain aloof, to pretend you don't know who they are, or that, if you do, you just don't care. At this point I cannot stress enough the importance of acting dumb.[*] Some footballers crave anonymity – it creates the 'chase' for them all over again,

[*] *In all kinds of situations, not just this. More of that later.*

something they rarely have to do now. So don't, for goodness' sake, think that by telling him your dad loves him or you had a poster of him on your wall when you were younger that it will endear you to him – it will not! Do you not think he's heard that a million times before? You may get a kiss, or even sex, out of sympathy, or maybe a depraved fetish on his part for sex with adoring fans. But you certainly won't get his number or ever hear from him again. Leave that stuff to the groupies.

Remember that song by The Streets? About how once men become famous it's so easy to get girls that they become bored? That's exactly what I mean! I know it can be hard, and it's taking a big gamble that they might just look right past you, but the night I met Wesley I managed to catch his eye by chatting to other guys and acting as if I didn't know who they were, not by throwing myself all over him. This worked quite naturally, as I *really* didn't know who they were. And the Primark? Well, I'm not sure how to explain the significance of that!

> *"A lady's imagination is very rapid; it jumps
> from admiration to love, from love to matrimony
> in a moment."* – Jane Austen

The night I met the footballer who would rather strangely change my life, Wesley, I was at my boyfriend's club in Kensington. It certainly wasn't a hotspot for footballers at the time, as they are essentially chavs at heart and you're better off trying your luck in the West End, Embassy or Faces in Essex. Remember, most footballers didn't even go to college as they're put into special schools straight after their GCSEs. (By special schools, I mean those that put emphasis on football skills ahead of academic talent. I don't mean they have special needs.) As you know, for the purposes of this book I'm calling my second footballer Wesley, as that's what he said his name was for almost the first month of our 'relationship'.

I was frequenting ***** on almost a weekly basis, along with my friends, as it was co-owned by my boyfriend, Club Boy. He hated me wandering off as I would invariably end up being chatted up by guys like Wesley, and so, in an attempt to put a stop to this, he tried to imprison me in the Champagne Lounge. Although this sounds fun, it was always full of hooray Henrys and Brendan Cole from *Strictly Come Dancing*, and the DJ never ever played Kanye West, even though I could see he had the CDs.

We had sneaked out and were walking around when a tall guy grabbed my hand and asked me to sit with him. I said no, as it would look beyond dodgy, but instead said that my friends and I would stay for a drink. And so I met Wesley. He was completely wasted but there was still something about him that I just found irresistible.

It may sound odd, but he was very *long*. I have a thing about long people, maybe because I'm long myself. If you knew who I was talking about you would notice how he just has the longest arms, hands, legs, everything! Apparently it's something to do with genes; you're attracted to people whose genes would make the best offspring with yours. My genes are telling me that I want long people. (My ex, Club Boy, was short, short, short! All over! Short little stubby arms and legs, short hands, short ... everything. I shan't bore you with the details.)

Club Boy would know Wesley was totally my type, so I busied myself talking to the more important guy at the table – the party organiser, who was short, pale and hairy. I would never look at him in a million years. At the time I knew that my boyfriend had me watched by security all over the club, and they knew what to look out for. By talking to this non-threatening little person, I knew I could stay in the vicinity and get to know Wesley better. Looking back, this was inadvertently one of the best things I could have done. Although I didn't know Wesley was a footballer at the time, since then I've used these tactics again – for research purposes only, of course! They are tried, tested – and true!

1. You don't want to look like you are there purely to talk to the footballer (which of course you may well be). This is way too obvious and it's what lots of girls do every single night.

2. It's important to get in with the promoter/organiser and befriend him – this worked especially well the first time, as he took my number and passed it along to Wesley the next day, when he was sober enough to remember who I was, who the Prime Minister was and what year we were

living in. (Sorry, I forgot for a second. He's a *footballer*. Of course he didn't know who the Prime Minister was.)

3. The footballer can't properly check you out if you're up in his face talking, or in a club more likely, shouting in his ear. (As my friend Kayla would say, "She was all up in his grille!" She's a bit gangster but I love it.) If you're across the table he can check you out without you noticing for a good few minutes. If you're engaged in animated conversation with a friend of his, someone he deems worthy of his company and friendship, he will automatically respect you as more of an equal than the many sluts who try to get a response on first meeting him. After all, when you've only just met someone, how much is there to talk about? The obvious things are, "What's your name?" "What do you do for a living?" Neither of these may you ask.

4. Sometimes the best route to the guy you want is the most indirect one. This works not only with footballers but with all guys. No, I take that back actually – with regular guys they might get jealous and think you like their friend. The footballers have big enough egos to handle it. So play the game. You might think it's risky, but remember – if you follow this guide he's not the only footballer you're ever going to meet, and if it doesn't work consider yourself to have had a lucky escape!

5. Essentially footballers are men. Men (and especially pro-sportsmen) are competitive. Men love to chase. Let him chase you! This is the single most important thing you can do.

FIRST STEPS

"A man can sleep around, no questions asked,
but if a woman makes nineteen or 20 mistakes
she's a tramp." – Joan Rivers

It's the morning after the night before, and if you followed my
advice last night you met a footballer.

Of course you did. You were in the right place at the right
time. He noticed you because you were wearing the right
things and knew how to act. You *did not* end up in a five-way
roasting session, and by that I don't mean a hearty Sunday
lunch. Oh, and you certainly didn't compromise yourself by
having sex with him on the first night. Did you?

Back when I met my first footballer in Newcastle, the next
morning I received an anonymous text – 'Morning Sexy' –
from one of those numbers you have to buy, because once you
see it it's instantly memorable. Was it Paddy? When I replied
and asked who it was, the response sent me into shock. It was

the name of one of the footballers! (We'll call him 'the Footballer'.) It slowly dawned on me that I'd been snared! Paddy was talking to me all night because the Footballer had told him to get my number – I couldn't believe it. I felt so stupid, so used, so … GREAT!

Why hadn't the Footballer come over and spoken to me himself? Oh, hang on. I think he tried, but I was busy with Paddy … maybe Paddy really had liked me but had to give me up to the Footballer. Which doesn't seem fair, but maybe that's his job. The whole thing was so seamless that he effortlessly fooled me – how many girls does he do this to? The Footballer must have a big … ego to assume they will all fall at his feet the moment he texts them.

I fell. Hard.

It all started out like some crazy made-for-TV Channel Five film: A young girl goes out and meets a famous man; *he* tracks *her* down – he is texting and calling her *all day*. (Literally. It was a seven-hour journey home and I didn't get to put my phone down once!) It's all a bit surreal: *Why is he texting little old me? OK, so I do have a pretty good bum, I'm always told – and I do have 33" legs. Hmmm, maybe I could pull this off!*

Texting – Make It Count!

The initial text is very important to the future of your relationship. At that moment you're just a texter. Most footballers, even married ones, have texters on their phone.

They're women the guys have met on a night out who entertain themselves by engaging in lengthy text convos and picture message swapping.

But you're more than a texter. You want to turn that text into talk, and that talk into action. Bad texts = bad response or no response. Good texts = lots of fun to be had! I'm not only judging this from my own experience. In writing this book I've spoken to lots of other women who have been in the same situation. They all agreed that texting played a huge part in their relationship – particularly the initial stages. Not only is it necessary to form a bond of trust between you (which in these times of kiss-and-tell frenzy is really needed) but it's also a lot of fun!

Be sure that your texts give a nice visual image as men – especially simple men such as footballers – are extremely visual creatures. If he asks you what you're doing, or if you've texted enough for one day and are signing off, don't just say, *"Right – I'm going to watch* Eastenders *now."* Turn it into something much more interesting or seductive, like:

"I'm so sleepy, am in bed now … naked [this bit is optional] – sweet dreams x"

or

"Okay, speak later, I'm off to the spa with my friend for a good workout, relaxing swim and steam."

The first will make him think of you in bed, you in bed will make him think of being in bed with you. Being in bed with you will make him think of sex – *ta da!* It's sexy, but not in a *"cum in yo a**, bitch"* type of way – it's subtle and sweet!

The second shows him that you have a life other than just texting him, you're out with your friend *and* you're working on your fit body. He'll definitely appreciate you taking care of yourself – particularly as he's so fitness-conscious himself. It also gives a better mental image than you moping about in your pyjamas (even if that really *is* what you're doing!). Think of yourself as one of those middle-aged housewives who save for their children's college fund by taking premium-rate chat line calls at home. When the caller asks what they're wearing the answer is always some kind of clichéd leather/red lace combination, when they're really slobbing about in rags and cooking dinner at the same time.

It's important to point out that none of your texts have to be strictly 100 percent true. If you're going shopping don't mention that you're going to Primark or Dagenham market. (I love it there! Chav City! My favourite pair of black skinny jeans, which I wear to death, came from there! £4.99!) Just mention that you got some really nice new underwear as your boobs seem to have gotten bigger recently, or something like that.

Here are some examples of common bad text messages and much better alternatives:

HOLIDAY
BAD MESSAGE:
"Where are you? What you doing? I'm soooo bored – wish you were here."
ALTERNATIVE:
"Hey! St Tropez is fantastic, I never want to leave! Weather is

so hot, I'm trying to get as few tan lines as possible if you know what I mean ... he he! See you when I'm back x"

The second message shows you're having lots of fun. By saying you don't want to leave, it indicates that you're not overly gagging to see him anytime soon. Don't send more than two messages during a one-week holiday. Mentioning the tan lines forces him to think about you oiled up in only a tiny pair of bikini bottoms. If he's having trouble with his imagination, send him a picture.

WORK

BAD MESSAGE:

"What u doing? I hate this shitty job, I wish I didn't have to work. I'm soooo bored. Text me back."

ALTERNATIVE:

"Hey! How's work? It's crazy-busy here but fun as always! Speak to you tonight, I'm off to a meeting now."

Show you're happy with your job, and therefore your life. You don't need him to change your life for you – you're happy with it the way it is, thank you very much.

NIGHT OUT:

BAD MESSAGE

"dkjsdlk I looove you – marry me so iiii can quit work and shooop all day – why u nooot answerint ur phone u hairyyy git?"

ALTERNATIVE:

That's right – nothing! Don't text him when you're on a night out. You're with your friends and you're supposed to be having fun with them, not sitting texting him. Write his telephone number down in your diary or on your mirror and delete it from your phone for the night. Not only is this a lot safer in case you lose your phone, it will also stop you drunk-texting him atrocious and highly regrettable messages like the one above.

On that note I must warn you about security. Firstly, get a lock on your phone to stop prying eyes, especially if your phone is lost. You would be surprised at what can happen when you don't have a lock.

Learnt My Lesson Story 1

About four months into my relationship with Wesley, I attended the London Club Awards with my boyfriend at the time (Club Boy) and got absolutely smashed on the free bar. (I mean on drinks from the free bar, not sitting atop the actual bar!) Unfortunately I don't remember the latter part of the night, but I'm told I had a great time and ended up at about 5am back at our hotel, the Royal Garden in Kensington.

We used to stay there every week as it was closer to town. He lived out in Surrey somewhere, and then Wimbledon after that, in an attempt at 'London living', but you know I don't sleep outside of Zone One.* Besides, they stock those cute little fridges at the Royal Garden with Lindt's creamiest milk

---

* Dammit! After moving out into Camden Town, which is clearly in Zone Two, I may have to rethink this rule. Okay, when staying with someone else/at someone else's expense, I will never sleep outside of Zone One. When paying rent I shall sleep in whichever zone I please!

chocolate and Appletiser (a surprisingly nice combination at 3:00am!), and they make the best breakfast croissants and strawberry jam in town.

Anyway, earlier that night I'd told Club Boy I'd forgotten my dress for the awards and had to go all the way back to Essex to fetch it. Really I was having a brief rendezvous with Wesley after work, as we hadn't seen each other in what seemed like ages. (In reality it was a little over a fortnight.) Club Boy offered to get his chauffeur, Yousef, to pick it up for me as he'd driven me to my house a million times before and could practically do the A13 drive in his sleep. (I think he probably did sometimes, as he took my friends and I home at 4am from parties.) I said it wasn't necessary, that I'd get it and be back in plenty of time for the awards.[*]

What a mistake-a to make-a. I had instantly made him suspicious. If offered, I always used the chauffeur car as much as possible, as walking is one of my least favourite things to do. Offering to go all the way back was totally out of character for me. Our personal chauffeur was almost number one on my Christmas card list, and I knew all about his wife and twin sons – this was how often he drove me.

Later that night, the awards were great and the after-party back at my boyfriend's club even better. As usual, I had surpassed myself and almost everyone else in terms of alcohol consumption – something that irritated Club Boy beyond belief. My drinking was one of the rare things we argued about, but I still got my own way. Every time I turned up with

* Obviously now I realise what a complete bitch I was, and I feel really badly about it.

my friends, a huge bottle of Grey Goose would be in front of me before you could say "permanent liver damage".

Later on that night I got back to the hotel and passed out on the bed, only to be woken up a few hours later by a very angry, and slightly sweaty, Club Boy. Despite me turning off my phone, taking the back off and hiding the two separate pieces in different parts of my bag, he had been sneaky enough to go through it all, put them together, work out how to turn it on and read my messages. *All* of my messages.

As with much of this book, I had not heeded my own advice. I only know all the tricks of the trade now through having learned the hard way. I hadn't saved him as 'Daddy'; I didn't have a lock on my phone. Chaos ensued. Strangely, all I cared about at the time was whether Club Boy had deleted Wesley's messages or his number, or whether he had called the number himself.

I didn't even really care that I had upset the man who adored me so much and continually gave me everything I wanted. That's how strong Wesley's hold was at this time. To give Club Boy his due, he hadn't deleted a thing, but instead asked me to do it myself. He also asked me to delete Wesley's number from my phone – it was becoming like one of Freddy Krueger's nightmares.

Luckily, Club Boy was a bit thick, so with a few swift manoeuvres I managed to change Wesley's name to something like Sophie. It was genius, considering it was all being done at 5:00am after the consumption of a larger than advisable amount of alcohol.

Learnt My Lesson Story 2

My friend Amelia let Wesley and I stay at her apartment a lot, and for that I will always be grateful. She had a top-floor flat in a beautiful old building right next door to where I worked in the centre of the City. She was extremely generous in letting me use it, and although I hadn't known her long I thought I could trust her. She even got me a set of keys to what she liked to call the 'Love Shack'. She didn't live there, but she was seeing an incredibly wealthy married man who worked in the area as a trader, stockbroker or something equally dull but lucrative, and he rented the apartment so he could see her at lunchtimes or *après*-office hours. The classic City Mistress.

It worked perfectly for the both of them. Amelia was a Swiss finishing school-educated, party-loving hell-raiser with a penchant for coke. She was totally spoiled by her dad until she grew up, and is now totally spoiled by the various doting men in her life. A complete *femme fatale*. Although I didn't envy her layabout lifestyle (I just *have to* work!), I had to give her credit for her incredibly liberated existence, and I was extremely grateful for the benefits that came with it – the flat's availability for mine and Wesley's trysts being one of them.

Amelia eventually got a steady boyfriend, something I never thought would happen, and wanted out of the sugar-daddy style relationship she had with Raef, the guy with the apartment. I begged her to stay with him but she really didn't want to. She asked me if I could get tickets to one of Wesley's games for her and her father, who was a massive fan – but I couldn't bring myself to ask him for something so groupie-ish. I explained that she wasn't going to have the flat for much longer, and asked time and again if he could find somewhere for us instead. Once, whilst in the throes of passion, he agreed to get a central London apartment (this was before I lived in London), but nothing ever materialised.

My friendship with Amelia became strained. Neither of us could understand why Wesley couldn't just get an apartment for us himself. It would have been loose change to him, but I think the commitment factor was scaring him. Eventually Amelia and I stopped talking almost altogether. I was a terribly selfish friend, but I just wanted to be with Wesley so much – and she was the one that was making it happen. Looking back, I was stupid. It's Wesley I should have been angry with.

Amelia and I went out one night as a last-ditch attempt to reconcile our friendship. As usual, I stayed at hers afterwards. A week later, the *News of the World* contacted me, telling me she had sold them our story. She had text messages, his number, the times we met, pictures, they had it all. I realised she must have got it from my phone while I was asleep.

So Rule #1 – get a lock on your phone! A locked phone is as much use to a thief as a glass of mineral water is to me at a Nikki Beach poolside. If a lock is not available on your phone, or you're just technologically retarded like I am, then save his number but *never* under his real name. A rather promiscuous (married) friend of mine once told me that she always saved her boyfriends' numbers under Dad Mobile. If anyone, particularly snooping husbands/boyfriends, has a quick opportunist look through your phone they're not going to waste precious time opening messages from your old dad.

This is also handy if you lose your phone. While most people rarely return lost phones anyway, the chances decrease to zero if they spot a famous footballer's number on there. They will also, without doubt, try to call him, and your footballer may think you've been handing his number out to people or have even sold it.

Frequency of texting varies greatly from footballer to footballer, or from man to man. With the first guy I met in Newcastle, he wanted to text *all the time!* I could barely keep up and made a point of not doing so. Footballers only train in the mornings, so they have a lot more free time than the rest of us. Wesley, on the other hand, could never really text during the day as he was with his child, but would always want to text late into the night – which was odd, as he lived with his girlfriend. I think that's why, when he eventually told me about her, I was ready to accept that they had a bad relationship and didn't even sleep together. Otherwise, how could he text into the early hours, every single night?

In texting, less is more. Never send more than two unanswered texts – remember he may have other factors affecting his life that are preventing him from getting in contact. I know it can sometimes be hard, but it's good to have a little written reminder to look at every time you feel like sending an unnecessary text. Mine was rather randomly written on a little card I got from Nikki Beach – so looking at it cheered me up straightaway! I kept it in my diary and wrote on the back:

The 'Wesley' Gospel

"It's not your fault – it's so frustrating that I can't see you more often. I think about it all the time and us texting all the time is making it even harder. Xxxx"

This was followed by:

READ THIS BEFORE SENDING A TEXT – YOU **WILL** REGRET (in a little box)

The first part of the above was a text he sent me once that totally put my mind at ease. I hadn't appreciated how hard it was for him to text freely. I even got annoyed with him when he texted me during the rare times I saw my boyfriend – so I can imagine how he felt. Once I read this to myself, I would almost always go back and delete the message I was about to send. It works a treat! My sister's friend used to save 'his' name as 'DO NOT TEXT' – when she went to hit 'send', it really did make her think twice.

As I've said, men are very visual creatures. Women appreciate words much more, the amount of kisses and the words used in texts mean a lot to them. Men just want the dreaded picture message!

The Devil's Lens – Picture Messaging

*"They used to photograph Shirley Temple through gauze.
They should photograph me through linoleum."*
– Tallulah Bankhead, veteran Hollywood actress

Now we all know that camera phones don't possess the most flattering lenses. Remember, girls – camera phones are not your friend! However, like most enemies it's best to keep them close and find out how to make them work for you. I've sent Wesley enough semi- (okay, and maybe some fully) naked pictures of myself to take a degree in it. (If there was such a thing as a degree in naked phone-picture-taking, that is.)

"What's the use of being naked if no one can see it?
Everyone loves a naked person. If you do something
naked – whatever it is – it is so much more fun."
– Chris Pontius, *Jackass*

"Sometimes you have to show a little skin. This reminds
boys of being naked, and then they think of sex. Anything
you can do to draw attention to your mouth is good."
– Cher, *Clueless*

"I need some pics I haven't seen you for a while x"
– Wesley, by text

Francesca's Golden Rules for Picture-Messaging a Boy

1. Never do it totally naked – that's not nice. If they want to see that then they can make the effort to come see it for real. If you relent and exchange *lots* of pics then there's not really anywhere else to go, so tastefully implied/legs-closed *Playboy* style is allowed.

2. Always use a fake tan/body makeup – it doesn't have to be all over, just the area you're taking a picture of. I only ever fake-tan the areas of my body that are going to be on show – it makes for an embarrassing moment if you end up getting naked in public though …

3. Use contouring to define curves – you could even use brown eye shadow for this, and Shimmer for that added pizzazz. Lots of more advanced tanning salons use contouring now to make waists seem skinnier, legs longer and busts bigger. Be bold! Remember that whatever you do in real life has to be x3 to show up in pictures.

4. If your face is going to be in them (which, for revealing pics, I always think is a bit risky – you never know when it could end up on YouTube or Facebook) then make sure you definitely multiply your makeup by three. Even if it looks ridiculously thick in real life, on camera it will just about be visible.

5. Wear nice underwear. This should be a given. Men – especially simpleminded men like footballers – seem to only like really plain and simple stuff. If you're blonde, go for black; if you're a brunette, go for cream or white. Anyone can get away with pink.

6. I know they probably won't really be looking, but don't have a skanky background with piles of washing and your mangy cat on show. Go for something simple like a cream wall or door.

7. Always take a picture of yourself via a mirror – never, ever should it be straight on. Mirrors give you the benefit of

more control over the angle, and a bit more distance between you and the camera lens. Close-ups are not called for here.

With these tips you just *can't* go wrong!

FIRST CONTACT

In the process of writing this book I've often referred back to my blog, *Essex Girl in London*, which I wrote back in 2006 when I first met the Footballer. I thought it would be good to include some of this, which is in the italic script you occasionally see.

Even though it was just two years ago, I cannot believe I wrote that stuff for the whole world to see. Oh the shame! I also can't believe I'm publishing it again now – but then this whole book is about being on a journey. I've come a long way since then, and I can see now that with him I was just a bit starstruck and couldn't believe a guy like him could be interested in a girl like me. (Please note that this was before I was a double D and had discovered the joys of fake tan!) Now I can see it was just a little fling that didn't really mean too much.

About a year and bit after I first met him, a journalist did a story on me in a particularly racy Sunday tabloid. The story was that I was selling my old breast implants on eBay (well, I was), and he took pictures from my Myspace which, stupidly, wasn't secured at the time. He published the story without my knowledge, named the Footballer and it was all just really, really tawdry. The Footballer didn't really speak to me after that – I think he felt I broke his trust. It's a shame, as he always used to ask about the book I'm now finally writing and demanded to be in the acknowledgements at the start.

But Wesley was a different kettle of fish. Whereas the Footballer just touched my body, Wesley touched my heart.

Now I'm older and wiser, I no longer think I was lucky to have had these guys in my life. It's more like *they* were lucky to know me, or maybe we're all lucky to know each other. This is how *you* should feel, girls. Still – for the purposes of this book I am including my old 2006 blogs, so go ahead. You read, I'll cringe:

OK, so the Boyfriend is gone and I am lost to a world of football. I turn up to work on Monday and ask a couple of the guys there if they have heard of the Footballer, of course they have and that's when I realise he is well and truly famous – I am immediately given facts, statistics and almost inside leg measurements as well as a whole host of links to pictures, stories and profiles of him. I can't believe it – I could walk up to any man on the street and about 80 percent of them could tell me more about this man of my dreams than I knew already.

We had been texting and speaking on the phone for almost

a month. The texts were fast and furious, often late into the night. He would call me at home and we would speak about all sorts of stuff – we had exchanged at least 500 texts during this time and several hours of phone conversations yet I knew virtually nothing about him. It's not that I wasn't interested because believe me I was! It's not like if you had just met a guy in a club – your first time of talking to him on the phone might go like:

Hey, so what do you do for a living? *(Don't tell me – I already know, and so does everyone I speak to. Do you think I didn't notice the queue of girls lining up to talk to you, do you think I haven't seen the hundreds of websites dedicated solely to your past and present career documenting every goal, every fall and every step? Do you think that now I know you I don't simply skip the back pages of* The Sun *where your face and name regularly appear for all to see?)*

So, what do you do in your spare time? *(Did you know that if I Google news stories I can tell exactly what you do in your spare time, I know when you got drunk, where and with who? It even had a story about you in the paper the other week for some misdemeanour or another.)*

As you can see it just doesn't work. That's why I find it so hard to speak to him sometimes – when he mentioned he's "got a match" there I was thinking – oh it's just a kick about with probably a few fans watching – after all it is a Wednesday night – not a stadium full of several thousand fans, full press turnout, live coverage on TV and a full report (with pictures, thank you Lord!) in the paper the next day.

This is big time – and I'm not sure I can blag not knowing just how successful and well known he is much longer.

You see my sister's the expert – she says that he has girls throwing themselves at him all the time – they research him and find out where he goes, they know his entire back catalogue and maybe he's fed up of that. I think what made him like me is the fact that I didn't know who he was – that's why for the first few weeks I made out I didn't really know what he did – I can't keep it up anymore – but how do you perfect the harmony between cool girl and groupie?

My day finally came – I could no longer hold out and pretend to be aloof – I gave in and met up with the Footballer on a Wednesday – I had done the commute to work (almost two hours) when he called me – just as I was walking into the office, he said he had a day off and as that doesn't happen very often he is back in his home town. It isn't very far from me and he begged me to go see him. Without a second thought I turned on my heel and went straight back home, jigging as I went! (I don't know what a jig is but I am pretty sure I was doing one that day!) I was sooooo nervous, after all I didn't even really speak to him that much on the night – this was going to be kind of a first date – although I knew there were going to be absolutely NO first date rules!

I got home and did some frantic Bridget Jones-stylee getting ready – did you know you can wash your hair, have a bath, shave your legs, moisturise and Sun Shimmer, do your makeup and straighten your hair in under an hour and a half if the motivation is strong enough?

Everything was going along so well I was ready early for my taxi! So what does a girl do when she's ready for some full-on bed action with one of the country's hottest sports stars? Puts on some Kanye West and dances around in her underwear of course! That's right – the bitch with the heart of stone actually danced she was so excited – about a man! I was more excited than the night before Christmas – and today I was due to get a BIG stocking!

Darn taxi was late getting to the hotel, errr ... yes hotel ... in the middle of the day ... a week day.

As I walked into the foyer there were about 20 businessmen in there and I had to go to the reception and ask to be taken to the Footballer's room. As I said his name as quietly as I could I could feel the stares burning into my back and suddenly became fully aware of what I looked like – the choices were grim:

a. Just another groupie – how many has he had up there this week?

b. An actual hooker.

I don't know which is worse!

I wanted to turn around and scream at them all that:

I'm not a groupie! I am not just at his beck and call because he's rich – HE chased ME! I have known him a month so this technically isn't even a first date! (not that a first date should ever be in a hotel room anyway) – don't judge me because of my Essex accent, my blonde hair and yes! These are FAKE! That doesn't automatically make me a gold digger who runs to do a kiss and tell in the News of The World *before she's even got out of the room! But you know what? I AM about to go and spend some serious hours NAKED with a hot guy that half your wives would trip over you to get to – so save your judgements for them, not me!*

Of course I didn't and instead went up to the room to meet my fate – and what a fate it was!

He met me at the door and I instantly noticed how tall he was – and how muscular and good looking ... sorry! My nerves quickly dissolved into "get me in that room – now!"

We chatted for a bit but it was obvious why we were both there and now I was glad that we were in the privacy of our own room. It was just minutes before we were taking each other's clothes off.

His body was perfect and he is the most well endowed man I have ever met – how did THIS never leak out onto the Google findings? A girl should be warned.

Take your hand off this book and stretch your arm out – now if you're a girl like me, I am not joking, it was about the same size as my arm from wrist to elbow.

I had a great time; I had a great time three times ... in five hours.

I had kind of hoped once meeting him today that my little (major) crush would end. After all it's always the way isn't it – you admire someone from afar then once you have them it never lives up to the expectation right? WRONG! It was all I had hoped for – and then some.

I always wanted just a little ... bit ... more. I thought, right when I sleep with him that will be it – I will have achieved getting close to him – except it's never enough is it? Sleeping with someone means you might be in the same bed, might even be as physically close as two people can be – but emotionally you can feel as if you are completely alone.

Anyway I ended up leaving his bed that day on a complete high – I had had my ultimate fix of the Footballer – my biggest yet. As I got in the taxi to go home I couldn't stop smiling to myself and felt an urge to call everyone I know telling them all about it. Unfortunately the taxi driver was also interested – he kept asking me why I had been meeting HIM – how did I know HIM – he couldn't believe that HE had called up some cabs for us – then the ultimate insult – he said:

"I couldn't believe it when 'the Footballer' called up for two cabs – we raced to get there to see him – my mate Tony got to take the superstar and I got stuck with you."

Nice. But nothing could drag me down off my high!

I just hoped that this little rendezvous hadn't fuelled my longing for him even more – because it felt like a dangerous game to be in – kind of like football where my heart is the ball, and I am now powerless to stop it being kicked.

When I think back to my first proper 'meet up' (read: bed-fest) with Wesley, I think of how little our relationship actually changed from that first date over the coming months, yet how differently I felt about him by the end. At this time we had been tentatively texting for just over a month. I say tentatively, as he obviously thought I must have known who he was (get over yourself, little boy!) and I thought that the texts were a trap set by my possessive boyfriend.

To be 100 percent sure that these flirty and sometimes dirty text sessions weren't going to lose all my free vodka, shopping and chauffeur rights, I made him call me so I could hear his voice and send me picture messages. I was convinced. He told me he was a personal trainer and a part-time stripper. The stripper thing put me off somewhat, but I never doubted him – he definitely had the right qualifications, if you know what I mean!

It was on a Friday night that I was supposed to be setting off to go see my sister, who lives in Lincolnshire. Wesley begged me to see him first, reasoning with me that I could stay there and continue my journey in the morning. Now there comes a point in every girl's day when she's faced with an ultimatum like this. Either she can haughtily decline and continue her day, safe in the knowledge that she certainly is not *that* kind of girl. Or, like me, and probably a lot of you, she can think, "Fuck it – willpower is not my strong point. Today just call me Miss Hussy, I'm going on a booty call and I don't care who knows it. I've not got laid in at least a month and I'm going to have fun. Abstinence is not my forte."

Anyway, I drove over to the address he gave me, which was his friend's apartment in Royal Docks. At the time, silly me thought that he was single and that he lived there. Naïve should be my middle name. Royal Docks is one of those completely characterless places in east London where flats go for mega-money – I have no idea why. The flat we stayed in belonged to a fellow footballer, but to this day I still don't know who. All I know is it was messy!

That night I pulled up to a huge, modern building reminiscent of an airport terminal – which isn't that odd, as City Airport was just down the road. I hated it. Give me a Victorian conversion in west London with high ceilings and sash windows any day of the week. But it was terribly easy to drive to – up the A13, turn off and I was there. And how much period architecture does one really need on a naked date?

I don't actually remember first seeing him. I just remember suddenly finding myself inside a huge apartment which was even blander than the exterior. All cream walls, cream carpets and cream furniture. A bit like a couple of wannabe property developers who watch too much *Homes under the Hammer* had come in, thrown a bucket of cream paint all over it and gone, *Ta-da!*

You could totally tell a boy lived there on his own. I just didn't realise it wasn't *my* boy. Later on he revealed how it was actually his friend's apartment, and that he lived in north London with his SHOCK HORROR NUMBER ONE: long-term girlfriend! And SHOCK HORROR NUMBER TWO: four-year-old child! I felt so disappointed. I couldn't believe I had fallen for it hook, line, sinker and nautically inspired tank-top. We sat on the cream sofa, next to the cream pouffe on the cream carpet, and he poured his heart out for over two hours about how he'd been with his girlfriend for years and things weren't going great.

She had got pregnant a couple of years ago with their child, who he didn't initially want, and now he felt more trapped than ever. He claimed they never had sex anymore, which was a bit too much information for me. I'm not Dr Phil – I didn't need to know this on what was technically our first date.

Romantic it was not. But in a way it was much more than that – he obviously didn't have anyone around him that he could talk to properly, and for some reason he felt he could talk to me. Or maybe he was just drunk.

We talked about everything from his job (all a fake – what a waste of sexytime) to where he came from. He was born in the ghetto – sorry, east London. When he was about ten his mum made him go stay with family abroad. He hated every second and had half of his belongings stolen by his cousins. All his shyness evaporated as he told me his childhood story.

It's strange, but throughout all of our months together and all of the things he said to me, this is what stands out most clearly. I felt like I was getting to see a side of him that no one had cared enough to ask about for a long, long time. I could tell he was really shy and introverted. He drank vodka from the minute I got there and tried to get me to drink too, which I'm genetically engineered to accept when proffered. He was stuttering and nervous for the first half an hour, but once he got talking about his life he seemed to totally change.

We'd been sitting up talking for about four hours by this time, and I was beginning to wonder when the trailers would finish and the main feature would start. We began discussing the picture messages and texts we had been sending each other more or less 24/7 over the last few weeks, and things began to hot up. I don't quite know what to write next, as this could quickly turn into graphically descriptive porn. Let me just tell you it was better than good! I would equate its pleasures with that of a whole tub of Ben and Jerry's Cookie Dough ice cream, or turning up at Paper to find Usher on the next table to you – which are clearly on a par.

About an hour later, we both laid back on the bed. We had moved into the bedroom by then, but I don't even remember how. It's like all those times when the last thing you remember is dancing atop table four in Chinawhite, before finding yourself in the back of a Bentley on the way back to your hotel – you have no recollection of how you got there.

Anyway, as we lay there and began talking again, the most dreaded thing that can happen to a girl transpired. No, one of my hair extensions hadn't somehow clipped itself to my armpit. This was much worse. He whipped out a picture of his baby.

Now why, boys, would you do a thing like that? I'm not talking about any guilt-related feelings, I just mean the pure ickiness factor!

Why, after having the hottest (illicit) sex of your life, would you want to see the result of said sex in the form of a tiny child with a fearsome face and crazy hair? It's the worst possible outcome of what you just did to me – and now you're showing it to me and I'm supposed to feign delight and interest?

There's only one baby I've ever encountered that I've found

remotely cute, and that's my friend Nic's. (She has a little boy called Harrison and I could eat him alive.) The rest can just crawl back up the uteruses from whence they came. I do not *need* some baby interrupting my weekly partying schedule and shopping time.

Back to the horrid picture. Would it have been impossibly rude to cover my eyes, and scream, "*La, la, la, la, la, I'm not looking!*"? It's like having unprotected sex with someone who then shows you a film of someone else dying of AIDS. (Like *Philadelphia* – how sad is that film? We used to watch it every Christmas in religious education for a 'treat'. Yeah, happy holidays!) Or persuading someone to eat a whole tear 'n' share to themselves, then showing them one of those gross documentaries they always show on Channel Five, like *Fattest Man in the World* or *Half-Ton Mum*. I was not impressed.

Whilst all this was going on in my head, I realised I had to show some kind of exterior emotion. I just managed a weak, "Aaaah – hasn't she got big ... hair? Cute!", whilst trying to tie a knot in my own fallopian tubes with mental power alone, a la Derren Brown.

I know these sentiments may seem a little harsh. Before I have pro-life baby lovers banging on my door, I should defend myself. I'm not totally anti-babies. I just thought it inappropriate at that particular moment in time.

100 percent ick.

DOING IT

"Ribbed for her pleasure ... eeeeiw!"
– Garth, *Wayne's World*

"You're going to have a lot of urges. You're going to want to take off your clothes and touch each other. But if you do touch each other, you WILL get chlamydia ... and die!" – Coach Carr, *Mean Girls*

I know we're all adults here but let's just get this out of the way quickly. When, uh, consummating your relationship, it's *imperative* that you use protection! Without sounding like an overanxious personal development teacher or your mum, it's just not worth the risk. These aren't any ordinary guys. They sleep around more than Russell Brand before his sex-addiction therapy, and have a habit of being really lax on the protection side of things.

I once went to a party with a Premiership footballer who also played in the US national team. In typical footballer fashion, after we'd been out a few times he passed my number onto one of his team-mates who had asked about me. Said footballer – who we will call 'Madrid', as that's the city where he played – began calling me non-stop, harassing me to fly out there with a friend of mine, Holly, to stay with him and the team.

I didn't have "charges by the hour" written on my forehead, so I refused, reassured that footballers really are Neanderthal men come back to earth for some noughties action. But he kept saying he wanted to talk to me, and boy, could he talk! I wouldn't have minded so much if I could make out what he was saying. Our conversations went something like this:

Madrid: YO! What up, ma? What's goin' down in London town?

Me: Hello ... (There's a crazy man on the phone!)

Madrid: Yo, bitch. (Apparently it's an affectionate term. Who knew?) Why ain't y'all and Holly comin' to see me? I wanna see my little snowflake! I can't wait! We gon' smack some shit up!

Me: Uh ... about that ... I don't think I can come ... I'm terribly busy with things in London and everything ... plus I don't even really know you that well.

Madrid: *Whaaaat?* I met you in London then we hooked up at the hotel for the afta' party! I told my boy, "She got a *fiiiiine* ass there!"

Me: Yes, I know, but still, we're not flying out there as we don't really know you.

Madrid: Y'all a grown-ass woman! Holly's a fine-ass woman! Y'all both grown-ass women! Come out here! Okay, well ... holla back!

You get the gist. Basically it was a lot of 'ass' talk and 'shizzle my nizzle'-ing. I found it near-impossible to locate anything coherent within all the ghetto-trash he constantly spoke! I managed to persuade him to get off the phone and continue the conversation via Facebook messenger, as I really couldn't understand a word he was saying. Luckily he was too slow or too lazy to type all the redundant words he'd littered his sentences with before, so things suddenly became a lot clearer. He continued to ask me to fly out there, then tried to entice me by saying we could "hang out at the hotel all day, sunbathing and having hot-ass lovin"! Needless to say, I found him very easy to refuse.*

> *"Hey babe seriousely though I want you to come to Spain. Would you come? Seriousely."*
> – ' Madrid', by text

He enquired as to whether I was on 'birth control'. (Found myself a real class act there, ladies!) I said that, although I was, it didn't make a difference. Protection is protection!

---

* *Dammit! Reading back on this some time later, I have to say that I changed my mind and we did go in the end! Read all about it in 'Research Results'.*

Then he came out with the classic line: "But I can't come with one of those things on." Lord, give me strength! If I had a pound for every time I, or one of my friends, had heard a footballer say that, I certainly wouldn't have to work for a living.

Why do guys always try and pull that one with girls who are on the pill? I don't take it because I'm getting promiscuous every night of the week – it's because it totally regulates your periods, so you can arrange hot dates, holidays and big events around them accurately.

Anyway, I guess my point is that, whatever the reason, if they don't care about their own health then they certainly won't care for yours.

> *"I don't do that shit."* – Ashley Cole,
> on allegedly being asked to wear protection by
> single mother Aimee Walton

An illustration of this came when I was seeing Wesley. He begged me to sleep with him without using protection as we had been seeing each other so regularly for so long. I could appreciate the sentiment, but what I found truly shocking was that he didn't *really* know me at that stage. I could have been anyone, as far as he knew back then. Luckily for us it wasn't the case. But theoretically I could have given him some horrible disease, which he in turn would have given to his girlfriend, the mother of his child. How he could ever have forgiven himself for that, I'll never know. I know that I could never forgive myself, if I was in his position.

WAG Don't-Wannabe

I read something like that once in a Martina Cole novel. (If you've not read her, you're missing out – big time!) In *Two Women*, one of the main characters contracts an STD which deforms and kills her unborn child; okay, she was raped on her wedding day by her dad, who got the disease from a hooker, so our cases aren't exactly identical. But you get my point.

The fact that he was so unconcerned with the health of his girlfriend and their child made me realise he had no respect for her, and even less for me. This is one of the reasons I'm such a WAG don't-wannabe today, and why I'm sharing all this hard-won knowledge with you, dear reader.

GOOGLING — STALKER-AID, OR PERFECTLY NORMAL RESEARCH TOOL FOR THE 21ST CENTURY GIRL?

Although us girls don't like to admit it, when we find a guy we *re-ee-eally* like, we're all a bit of a secret stalker. Not in a crouching-outside-your-house-in-a-balaclava kind of way, but rather in a pretend-I'm-working-and-worthy-of-equal-pay-to-men-while-really-I'm-googling-my-crush sense.

And what's wrong with that?

Googling is one of the best inventions known to womankind. And no, I'm not talking about researching how to buy a gift for under a tenner (www.tenbelow.co.uk), the life story of a past King of Lebanon or how to get rid of fleas – I am talking about man-Googling!

For any savvy girl about town these days, Google is the ultimate weapon in her dating armoury – that is, of course, if her man's Googlable. Lots of girls these days rate a man's worth by his Googlability. If you tap in your beloved's name and nothing comes up, what does that tell you? If he's not worth writing about then he's not worth sleeping with.[*]

(Oh, and by the way, here's another general tip I've picked up. When dating someone it's always good to check them out on Credit Gate. That way you can see if he really is a company director, check out his company and its registered address. A quick and easy way to suss out who's trying to dupe you.)

After meeting the Footballer (we're back in 2006 now – do keep up!) there was so little I knew about him, and *sooo* much I wanted to learn! I found Google, and took my first steps on the path to stalkerdom. As I typed his name into the little box, an information superstore popped up with everything I could ever wish to know – and more!

I revelled (in the office, I'm not so sad as to do it at home!) in pages and pages dedicated to him, and soon found out his career history, his middle name, even his height and weight! Every kick, every match and every goal were all recorded. I soon discovered the delights of Google images and Google news, updated with new stories about your man every single minute. (If he's popular enough, that is.) It's surprising how many people update websites and blogs about sportsmen and celebrities all day long. Where *do* they find the time?

The problem with Google, of course, is that it's slightly addictive – and it's just not natural. With your average guy you meet in a wine bar, or at your favourite club, you can be on even ground. You go out on dates and get to know each other

[*] *Apparently.*

slowly. What happened with the Footballer is that I found a massive chocolate cake of information about him. I couldn't help myself, and gorged the lot. I ended up feeling sick, as with everything I now knew about him I felt like a fake.

How can you act like a ... (I hate to use this word!) ... *fan* (shudder), and sign up for a Google alert so that every time a new story about him is published a little message pops up in your inbox? Maybe you even type his name into eBay? But how can you obsess over him in the way a fan does over a celebrity but still act normally with him in real life? It's nigh on *impossible!*

So which do we give up? The Google addiction or the Footballer?

Top Half-Dozen Wrong Things I Have Done on the Internet since Meeting the Footballer

(Just to confirm – I *am* ashamed of these, a lot! Just because I'm a cool cat now doesn't mean that I wasn't once a bit of a geek, all the way back in 2006. This book wouldn't be true to itself if I left out the cringe-worthy bits.)

1. Googled him and found out every statistic and report written on him – ever.
2. Signed up to Google alerts for a 9am fix of the Footballer.
3. Drooled over Google images of him for several minutes.
4. Researched news stories like Poirot on heat and found out some dodgy secrets and a somewhat shady past.

5. Put his name into eBay and looked at all the stuff you can buy connected with him ... if some of it happened to slip into my shopping basket blame my dodgy mouse, not me!*
6. Joined his fan club. No, I'm kidding – that really *is* sad! Don't boost his ego any more than necessary – these findings are SECRET! Do not leave a trail. Don't leave messages on forums, or join any sites.

Staying with this IT-related theme, let me just tell you about networking sites. Facebook and Myspace are great for just that – networking! Lots of people just use them to catch up with old schoolfriends they hate, old friends who have got fat or ex-boyfriends they'd rather forget – but there's so much more to gain from them.

Lots of promoters, party planners, footballers, actors and, well, Russell Brand all scour profiles as much as any computer geek. It's a great way to get to know new promoters, and I once even went on a date with a footballer who played for ******* or something (research, you understand) after hooking up on Myspace. (Looking back, it really doesn't seem like something I would have done, but I can't think how else I would have met him.)

Internet dating is no longer a taboo subject. Remember when Chip, *Napoleon Dynamite*'s brother, goes internet dating? (That's the funniest damn movie I've ever seen, and it has no relevance to this book at all!) It's a common way of

---

* *I'm totally kidding, okay? I wasn't that sad! My sister did get me a signed card thing of the Footballer as a joke Christmas present though. I laughed so much before deciding to use it as a bookmark.*

meeting people within your circles and totally acceptable to the average girl.

Even my quite conservative* sister met her fiancé through Dating Direct, an online dating service. She's really ashamed of it now, and is terrified of people at her wedding asking for some romantic story about how they met, so she probably won't thank me for mentioning it in a book. But she was 25, single, gorgeous, clever and funny, with her own successful business, but just could not find a decent man. All the local guys were intimidated by her and men she met through work in the City were too far up their own arses to notice her own very peachy model. In a last-ditch attempt (she won't like that either), she signed up and within a month had dated a popular sitcom writer, a pilot, a fireman and, finally, Elliott – the love of her life. Within a year she'd moved in with him, and they're still together now.

I'm praying for a wedding date to be set any day now, because this sister wants to be a bridesmaid! I'm hoping my abundantly charming wit will come across in this book, and she'll ask me to make a speech of some kind. (Do bridesmaids make speeches?) I rather fancy myself in a figure-hugging, hunter-green bridesmaid dress, clinking my fork seductively against my champagne glass and putting the wedding party in stitches with 'hilarious' anecdotes about my sister.

But to wrap this whole computer thing up – don't be afraid of using the internet to further your research. Knowledge is

---

Not in a rightwing kind of way, she's just relatively traditional. In fact she's very anti-Tory if you get her started about how Margaret Thatcher stole her milk.

power, and there's nothing worse than going into a situation unprepared or ill-informed. That's why Wesley angered me so much. He lied about everything. I didn't know whether I was seeing a footballer, or whether he was a family man, at least at first – he simply didn't tell me.

So Google away my friends, but beware – if you start to wear glasses, get pasty, spend your Saturdays hanging around PC World, or decline a night out at Chinawhite in favour of a night on the web – step away from that laptop!

Top Ten Frivolous Things to Spend a Footballer's Money on

Take a break and stop working so hard. If you've got a footballer knocking at your door (and I find that when one appears, about five more swiftly follow) why not momentarily take advantage of the situation? Here are my top ten means of helping him spend his money. After all, there's only so much pimp bling and Cristal one baller can buy.

1. Champagne – don't go for the footballer's clichéd favourite, Cristal. Recently it's been out of favour with a lot of people. (It was deemed supposedly 'racist', after the house said it didn't welcome the business of stars such as Jay-Z.) So try the classic Krug Grand Cuvee. This champagne is fermented in a small oak cask which gives it a distinctive taste. If you really want to splash out try their new Clos d'Ambonnay, which is a mere £780 a glass.

2. Buy a pair of Gina shoes from Harrods' Shoe Boudoir. It's like shoe shopping in your bedroom! Gina shoes are all handmade and incredibly comfortable – not to mention sparklier than a WAG's wedding ring!

3. Go to Nikki Beach in St Tropez for an entire weekend. You'll love their poolside white beds and fabulous cocktails. The weekend's not complete if you don't get sprayed with champagne.

4. Eat Kobi steak. It's made from Wagyu cows, which are like the royalty of the cow world. They each have a personal butler who massages them daily, and they even drink beer! Ninth-grade gold-style is the best you can buy. Try it – I defy you not to love it!

5. Stay at the Dorchester. For a month. Do nothing but watch movies and eat from their fabulous room service. Venture downstairs and drink at China Tang once a day. Trust me, it's perfect.

6. Go to Mo*Vida and order Britain's most expensive cocktail. The Flawless cocktail contains Angostura bitters, Cristal Rose champagne, Louise XII cognac and edible 24-carat gold leaf, which is all served in a Swarovski crystal glass. The best bit? Each cocktail comes with an eleven-carat white diamond ring in the bottom. Oh, it also features a £35,000 price tag too.

7. Get him to hire out an entire club for your birthday and book Usher to sing, 'Happy Birthday' to you. I went to a party where that actually happened; it was madness. (On second thoughts, I would *so* prefer Kanye West!)

8. Get him to buy you a Maybach. Not because they're hot – because they're so *not* – but just because you can.

9. Moan about your 'future financial security' and say you would feel much safer living in an apartment on Park Lane. With the deeds in your name.

10. Pay someone – anyone – £20,000 to have a tattoo spelling your name in big capital letters. (Why not? Besides, I couldn't think of a number ten!)

COPING WITH 'THE KNOWLEDGE'

'The Knowledge' is one of the most underrated aspects of a relationship with a man adored by millions, yet also the hardest.

The Knowledge is what I call it when you know so many personal things about someone who's well-known to the point of being idolised, but you just cannot tell anyone as you have to 'respect their privacy'. (For which read: cover up their dirty little secrets, like their fetish for spanking … oops, did I just say that?)

You may want to tell the whole world, but resist the temptation. I find it useful to write a diary instead. If my heart is so passionate that it feels like it's on fire, if it's so happy that it feels like it could burst, or so sad that it could break and scatter into a million pieces, then I let out all my emotion on paper.

Maybe that's not enough, and you want someone –

anyone – to know. Then in this case an online (and anonymous!) blog will do the trick. I enjoyed writing www.essexgirlinlondon.blogspot.com so much and got loads of great feedback, even girls asking me for advice. Just ensure that you always change names, dates and places, so that nothing is traceable, and write it under a pseudonym. I called myself 'Essex Girl in London' as I felt I was living a very split life at the time. It was when I very first started to sample the delights that London has to offer, but was too scared to move here and thus was living halfway back in my old life.

At the time my life was so separated that I was almost like two different people. I'm talking like Kerry Katona now, but luckily I'm not bipolar or anything. Like lots of young people, I made mistakes and did things that I might be ashamed of now – maybe that's why I didn't want to feel like 'me'.

For a while I would shorten my name to just 'Amber' when I was in London. This was partly because, in loud clubs, it was easier for people to hear than 'Francesca', and partly because, when people would call or text me and ask for 'Amber', my drink-fuddled brain could at least place which county I'd met them in. But mostly it was because I didn't always have to be Francesca, who was normally quite shy and reserved, and would never do anything on her own.

This 'Amber', who I had created, was a million miles away from the somewhat lanky smalltown girl who spent every weekend with her old childhood friends and her horses. Amber was bold and confident; she dated men from all walks of life, from cultured oil or shipping heirs to footballers.

Amber was most comfortable in Michelin-starred restaurants, top casinos and private members' clubs, partying with newfound friends who were 'models' or socialites.

In the end my long-term boyfriend (nine months is long-term for a commitment-phobe like me, okay?), Club Boy, even called me Amber. We used to take my mum and sister out to dinner sometimes and they would be calling me Fran, or Francesca, and he would be calling me Amber. Anyone overhearing us must have thought I had some complex personality disorder. (Looking back, maybe I did!)

People rarely call me Amber now. I only use it when I'm somewhere noisy and someone pesters me for my name who I don't want to talk to. Or sometimes I say my name's Dave. That soon scares them off!

When it comes to dealing with the Knowledge, it's always good to have a trustworthy friend to pour your heart out to. Sometimes things get all too much, and you need someone to talk to who knows exactly what's going on. Fortunately, when things with Wesley got tough towards the end, I had a close friend to turn to. One night, near the end of our relationship, I had met up with him at the flat to tell him about the predicament I was in with Amelia and the *News of the World*.

But as I tried to get the words out he started telling me about how he felt his life was falling apart all around him. He was badly injured; his primary relationship was on the rocks and a close relative had just died, to top it all off. He was really upset and I just couldn't add to his problems. I still really cared for him, despite all the crap.

I met my confidante afterwards and I just cried as I explained it all to her. Then she cried too! It was a very emotional time and I was in turmoil. If I didn't have the emotional release of a friend and my diary, I don't know what I would have done.

It sounds a little dramatic, but it really was quite an ordeal. At one point a few weeks later, Wesley's lawyers were so worried that I might do something crazy, like kill myself, that they advised me to get rid of my phone, not to return home to Essex, to stay in a London hotel and then to travel the world. All of this was to be on them.

Silly little me chose to decline this offer in a last-ditch attempt to resurrect our fragile 'relationship' – and to prove that I didn't want anything from him. How dumb was I? At the time I thought I was being noble and good, proving to him that I wasn't in it for his money. But looking back – *shit!* I could have LIVED on Nikki Beach for a month. Better still, I could have made a world tour of all the Nikki Beaches ever created, from Marbella to Miami. I could have hired the infamous Serena Cook, the ultimate Balearic fixer, to sort me out an unforgettable fortnight in Ibiza Town. I could then have wasted February in the Eagle Club on Wasserngrat in Gstaad, staying in the Palace Hotel without having to set foot on a cold, nasty ski slope. As Vassi Chamberlain of *Tatler* once said, your social life can only go downhill if you don't do Gstaad. Damn! *Double damn!*

WAG Don't-Wannabe

I guess the point is, no matter where you go in life and what you're doing, never underestimate the importance of your friends. I'm lucky to have had a really close-knit group I could turn to ever since early childhood. There's nothing more comforting than an old friend who knows you inside out and loves you regardless.

I met Jennifer at the grand old age of three. She lived next door, and we enraged my mum by constantly picking a huge hole in her bush (it wasn't nearly as rude as it sounds) so that we could talk to each other.

I met Sophia on my first day of school, rather embarrassingly, just as I was crying and screaming whilst hanging on to my mum's leg, begging her not to go. It was also shortly after I'd wet myself in front of my teacher and the entire class. Amazingly, she still decided to be my friend, and we were in the same class from ages four to sixteen. Even though we went to different colleges and now live in different counties, we go on holiday together every year and I couldn't be without her.

Likewise, it's great to have new friends for when you step away from your old life and into the unknown. For me, that was moving to London on my own, and it's been great to find kindred spirits in Kayla, Holly and Semi.

Kayla's the craziest girl I know, totally ghetto-fabulous, does everything at full speed. You never have a bad night out with her. Her full-time job seems to be sleeping on my floor, being hungover and dancing on tables with me most nights of the week. Holly's job description seems much the same. She's one girl in front of whom I can say or do anything and she won't judge me.

Semi is the sexiest boy I know, and is totally France's answer to Alfie. Women can't help but fall over themselves to spend time with him, and you would understand why if you ever got the chance to meet him. He's tall, dark, French and ridiculously good looking. Dare I say he's a Parisian Zoolander? (He hates me calling him that.) He's a promoter on and off in top London nightclubs, as he's got the looks and charm to pull in the girls – but he doesn't drink and he hates the scene, so I don't know why he does it. We had a short, hot fling last summer and have remained good friends since.

Sounds perfect, right, so now you may be asking why we're not together? Well, for starters he's a proper hobo (that does mean 'traveller', doesn't it?) and would never settle in one place. Secondly, he's incredibly aesthetically orientated. He once chastised me for going down the crisps and nuts aisle in Tesco because that's where the 'fat people' are, and expressed an extreme hatred for my little bedside alarm clock because it's 'ugly'. Nonetheless, I love him as a friend and he's been instrumental to my adapting to London life.

> *"If life gives you a lemon, make lemonade!"*
> – Mel B on her relationship with Eddie Murphy

This is my advice to you in the instance that a footballer or his solicitors offer you something: TAKE IT!!! Take it with both hands and take it quickly. If it's being offered to you, then it's been offered to 100 girls before you. (Okay maybe not 100, but at least one. And you certainly won't be the last.) Whatever you think you're going to prove by refusing isn't worth it. Although I was capable of loyalty to Wesley, footballers invariably are not and so I say – just TAKE IT!!!

Before any critics rush to claim I'm some trashy little gold-digger, let me just point out that our economy is erratic right now, with constant talk of the 'credit crunch', a looming recession and hundreds of people losing their jobs and houses left, right and centre. When people say that it's wrong to accept what amounts to a day's loose change from a footballer, in order to fulfil your ambition of travelling the world, taking a degree, setting up a business or buying a house, they should take a step back and look at the bigger picture.

I'm fortunate enough to work for an international charitable foundation which gives money to combat world poverty. I receive letters every day both from individuals in distress and national charities in dire need of funds. Did you know that the average hospice costs £6 million a year to run, and isn't fully supported by the government or the NHS, relying instead on donations?

I have had absolutely heartbreaking letters from people who have managed to get off the streets and into a house, only to find it's totally unfurnished and uncarpeted, with nails sticking out of splintering floorboards while their baby runs around the room. Some people need life-saving operations. One girl the same age as me wrote from Poland; she had a tumour on her spine and needed an operation costing

£35,000. Without it she was slowly being paralysed, and her fear was evident in the words she so bravely wrote to me.

Among the most heartbreaking letters are the most common ones: single mothers who can't afford the simplest of luxuries, a child's school uniform or a new bed; pensioners who don't own their own home and are threatened with eviction, or who are literally freezing as they can't afford fuel bills.

Away from the glitz and glamour I inhabit at night, these stories really bring me back down to earth. I can't help every single one of these people, but it's made me realise how lucky I am to be in control of my life and my finances. A lot of people in desperate situations used to be just like me, young and carefree.

Who knows if that will change with the arrival of an unexpected child, or sudden ill health? I don't ever want to have to beg at the Citizen's Advice Bureau and to write dozens of letters just to scrape together enough money for my electricity bill, only to be plagued with the same problem again next month.

And so you may scorn me for advising you to use any situation to your financial advantage, but I can clearly see the other side of what could happen. As American football player Clinton Jones once said, I've never been in a situation where having money made it worse.

Enough serious stuff! If your future is secured then just take the money and spend a month at Nikki Beach anyway! I could die just thinking about their breezy white canopies and fabulous cocktails ...

KISS-AND-TELL GIRL

"People everywhere confuse what they
read in the newspapers with news."
– A. J. Liebling, *The New Yorker*

Selling a story can be either the most liberating thing you've done, or the most demeaning experience ever. There's no rulebook, and trust me when I say *nobody* is on your side. In the following pages I've tried to give as much helpful advice as I can, having been there and done that.

The classic kiss-and-tell is not the ideal ending to your relationship, but sometimes it's the only way. I like to call it 'relationship insurance'. You see, men are like cars; a local boy you meet down the pub is less likely to cheat, humiliate, hurt or dump you – he's more like a reliable old Ford Fiesta, and so you don't really need any insurance against him breaking your heart. If he *does* do any of the above, you can always exact your own little revenge (if really necessary) by way of Facebook or Myspace – but you know that anything you stand to lose is minimal.

A footballer, on the other hand, is like a Ferrari or a Bugatti. If anything goes wrong it's going to be major and it will cost you a lot.

Okay, maybe that doesn't exactly make sense, but my point is this. When embarking upon a relationship with a footballer, be prepared for the high likelihood of him temporarily ruining your life. Your heart may be broken in ways you didn't even know existed, and you may be treated as little more than a problem to throw money at. (Catch, girls, catch!) And so you should take out your own personal relationship insurance.

INSURANCE POLICY NUMBER 46 26 27 19 22

Policy Holder:	Francesca Amber Sawyer
Age:	23
Occupation:	Writer and Author
Item(s) to be insured:	Heart and sanity
Against what risks:	Devious footballer 'Wesley'
Evident risks:	Habitual liar Live-in girlfriend Child under 5 years Been around the block a few times (allegedly) National adoration by both men and women More than 50 not very careful lady owners (estimate)
Risk:	High

Make a pact with yourself that, once your farcical relationship with whatever love-rat footballer you're seeing is never going to get any better, or is affecting your mental health, you will do something totally drastic and irreversible – like selling your story – thereby cutting all ties and making it impossible to go back to him. You may also gain your revenge into the bargain.

The reasons may be that you lose your job because of him; he is caught by the press dogging, or hiring prostitutes; he becomes more elusive than Bin Laden when the bill arrives at a dinner table. Any of these are classic examples. Reasons *not* to be used to justify kiss-and-tell include that he annoyed you one night, he doesn't want to carry on the relationship, or his wife or girlfriend has fallen pregnant. Under those circumstances, your fellow woman does not need any further stress.

As is the case with most women involved in an affair, my relationship with Wesley eventually started to ravage almost all aspects of my life. After it had been going on for six months, when my boyfriend (Club Boy) found out it broke his heart. He forgave me and we tried to continue, but I soon realised it wasn't worth it as he was constantly asking where I was, who I was with and what I was doing.

We broke up on pretty bad terms, but what pains me more is that I hurt a genuinely sweet, unselfish man who would do anything for me. If he ever reads this book, I hope he knows that I am genuinely sorry and all the jokes about his sweaty hairiness are just that – jokes.[*] Not only had I lost my steady relationship, but my friends and family were frustrated as they could see what a mess I was becoming, and that I couldn't handle keeping half of my life secret. They begged me to stop the charade, but by that time I was powerless to.

What hurts me most of all, in retrospect, is how I used Amelia. She selflessly gave us the use of her home so that we could see each other and I'm very much aware that, without her help, we would never have got so far in our relationship. But things became strained as both Wesley and I relied on her more and more to sustain our illicit affair. It was this that eventually led her to selling us out to the *News of the World*. (She has still never admitted to me that it was her, but they showed me an affidavit that she'd apparently signed.)

The newspaper contacted me via a journalist I had done a few features with in the past. They had everything on us – they knew where and how we met, when we saw each other and how long it had been going on for. There were even paparazzi shots of him and me entering and leaving the apartment building! They also had various other scandalous details which only a close friend like Amelia would have known.

They were all set to do a story the very next week and were champing at the bit to get me involved. Wesley is an international player and quite a prominent figure in English football, with a reputation as a quiet family man. (Ha!) This was a big story for them. Over the next few days I was called,

---

* *Some girls really like a hirsute gentleman. It reminds them of the loving relationship they had with their first pet. (Sorry, I can't seem to stop now that I've started!)*

texted and emailed constantly. I was pressured into meeting up with one of their journalists and signing a confidentiality agreement which meant that I couldn't tell anyone else about the affair.

With the help of my journalist contact they talked me around into thinking that I could actually 'help' Wesley by making the story less damaging. When I called them in tears one morning, begging them to stop the story, my 'friend', who I shall call G, calmly informed me that I was too far in and that the only way I would have any control would be to work the story to my advantage. G kept telling me that the paper would go ahead with or without me – but without me they would make me sound like an absolute slut and totally ruin Wesley's life. If I worked with them, I would somehow regain a kind of control over proceedings. Or so I was told.

This sort of pressure isn't uncommon with tabloids – they're desperate to get their scoop and often use advanced pressure tactics to press-gang[*] girls into complying with them. G was instrumental in the newspaper's attack on me; their thinking was that if they had one of my friends onside I would be more compliant. They were right, I guess.

One night I had (stupidly) confided in him my suspicions that Wesley's girlfriend was pregnant again. He'd been really upset the last time I saw him and said that something bad had happened – then he backtracked and said that it was 'kind of good'. It also meant that, for a short time, we wouldn't see so

---

[*] I almost said 'gang-bang' there. Being as this is a book about footballers, that phrase seems somehow more apposite than press-gang.

much of each other, but he wouldn't tell me why. The only obvious possibility was that 'she' was pregnant again. Soon after I told G this, he called me at my office and told me that a certain newspaper had just had a tip-off that it was true, and that I should definitely forget any reservations I had and just go ahead with it.

I was devastated. At this point Wesley had told me that they hadn't had sex in months and barely spoke. Today, many months on, no baby has ever materialised. It all seems like a complete fabrication to lure me in. But what I had in fact managed to do, without even intending to or realising it, was to break up their relationship.

So even people you trust will deceive you to get at the story. The important thing to remember is that, whenever you're dealing with people who want to make money out of you, no one is your friend. When I was going through all of this with Wesley, he was only interested in preserving his public image; his lawyers wanted to protect their client; the newspapers wanted their story – no one actually cared about what I wanted or what happened to me. Everyone was nice to me as they wanted to keep me sweet – but I could trust nobody.

I buried my head in the sand for the rest of that week, telling myself that I would tell Wesley the week after. But really, I was just desperate not to be a disappointment to him.

Meanwhile, I was getting myself deeper and deeper into the mess and finding it hard to keep my sanity. In the end I actually managed to get out of the *News of the World* situation with the help of Wesley's lawyers, of all people! About a month after that, after much deliberation, I went to *The People* and told the story my way – leaving Wesley anonymous.

"Why? Why would you do it?" – Wesley, by text

A lot of people ask me why I ever did a kiss-and-tell on Wesley if I supposedly cared for him so much, and why I've never named him. Neither answer is simple. Firstly, I never *chose* to go to the papers about our relationship. They approached me and, until you've had the press badgering you, you cannot imagine what the pressure is like.

So I later decided to make the best of a bad situation. Since gathering research material for this book, I've now become surer than ever that cutting off all ties with him was the best decision I ever made.

Purely for research purposes, you understand, I decided to transform myself (temporarily) into a WAG-wannabe, in order to get some first-hand experience. I have to say that all my fears about these guys have been more than confirmed, but more of that later …

Much upheaval, many irate text messages and one disastrous Christmas party later, I eventually turned my back on Wesley and went ahead with *The People*. I wanted to sever all ties with him forever, wrongly believing that, having sold my story (surely the ultimate betrayal in a footballer's eyes), he would never want to see me again. Although this was true for a while, he's actually been back in contact with me twice since – the latest occasion being only last week.

I couldn't believe he would be willing to go through all this again. Surely I am one of the highest risks – along with broken metatarsals – currently known to a footballer in this country? When they sign up to a club, I'm sure they now get a little welcome pack with my angry face on it, warning, "DO NOT GO NEAR THIS GIRL – SHE IS ANTI-FOOTBALLER AND SHE WILL USE YOU (and your hot body) FOR THE BENEFIT OF RESEARCHING ARTICLES AND BOOKS."

As for not naming him, well, that's a personal choice. If I was out to do a basic kiss-and-tell, then yes, okay. But this isn't about naming and shaming. There are things which only Wesley and I know to this day, things that, if I'd chosen to reveal them, would have landed him in the biggest heap of shit you can imagine. But I haven't ever been *quite* angry enough at him to want to do that. At the end of it all, he still has a child who is going to look up to him and doesn't deserve to have the squalid details made public. And besides, the story I have to tell spreads far wider than simply the name of one guy.

But don't be afraid of that phrase, 'kiss and tell'. It's not always a bad thing, and sometimes there's no better way to solve a problem than with a front-page story. Speaking personally though, I feel that mine was not so much a kiss-and-tell as a 'pick me up/put me down/lie to me/seven-month affair/heartbreak and tantrums/interrogation by your lawyers and unfair demands/screw you, I'm ending this the only way

I know how!/but I'm not so heartless as to name who you are/I don't want your child to know' story.

Much more fitting, but not quite as catchy, perhaps.

Selling Your Story, or Selling Your Soul? (The Press Can Be the Devil)

When you decide to kiss and tell, the first thing you have to think about is what you have to lose personally or professionally. (Or what you have to gain, I suppose.) Probably at the forefront of your mind is your particular beef with the footballer in question. Both of these determine what kind of kiss-and-tell girl you are.

Type One is your typical Alicia Douvall character. Now there's nothing wrong with being a media whore; I've sold more harmless stories on many and various subjects than I've had hot dinners, and it can be very lucrative. Alicia, for her part, is a single mother who's managed to work the system to her advantage. Good for her!

Type One are girls who have met a famous guy that night, had some sort of interaction with him purely for the sake of a story, then gone and sold it the very next day solely for money (or fame, if they're that naïve). They get an incredibly clichéd bad image, which is perhaps unfair. Basically they're honey-traps, and the girlfriend or wife of the love-rat involved should be shaking the girl's hand – not slating her. She may well just have been saved from decades of pointless marital heartache.

Although, in a strange and twisted way. I appreciate what

they do and why they do it, it's not what I've ever done personally.

Type Two is yours truly, and the many, many other girls I've seen make the Sunday tabloids over the years. Girls who have simply fallen in love. They've had a long-term relationship with the guy in question and sold their story as a last resort, as the only way to break their ties to the man. I can totally understand this, and have nothing but compassion and respect for the girls that do it.

One story I saw the other day really struck a chord with me. Her name was Stephanie and she had been secretly seeing Jermain Defoe for SEVEN YEARS! Can you imagine? I had my affair with Wesley for seven months and that changed my life enough to make me write this book. Jermain is in a league of his own and, during this time, had more than two fiancées. The poor woman shared the delusion of thousands of women in dead-end affairs or relationships: one day, he was going to be with her for good. Sure.

Remember this: The way you start a relationship with a footballer – or with any man for that matter – is invariably how you will end it.

Stephanie said at the end of the article how devastated she was to suddenly awaken from his spell and find herself, aged 30, a single mother, wasting her life on a dead relationship. I actually cried for half an hour when I read that, and her face still haunts me now.

Hell, that could have been me!

Are you ready?

TABLOID TALES - THE LOGISTICS

Please be aware, girls, that when undertaking a kiss-and-tell it will take over the next few weeks of your life completely. Be prepared to bare your soul, and probably your boobs – having done both, I know the first is much more painful. You'll be in two minds the whole time as to whether you're doing the right thing, even if (as in my case) you're doing it to finally break off the relationship. You will have to reveal every intimate detail of your sex life, often to total strangers, and let a photographer shoot the private messages on your phone. It can be soul-destroying, liberating and everything in between.

So, if you're prepared for it, let's get going!

Firstly you need to know how to approach the newspapers.

If you're confident enough to do it yourself then log onto a newspaper's website and you'll find links for contacting them.

Sometimes you may also see a relevant story which at the end will say, "Do you know a story about a footballer? If so, call us on …"

These are pretty straightforward methods that everyone can follow if they have little or no previous experience with the press. But remember, this is all about appearances and you don't want to be short-changed – so contact a particular individual for that personal touch. Find out the email format for the particular newspaper and apply to it the name of any journalist who you've seen do big kiss-and tell stories in a sensitive light.

Luckily, I suppose, I know quite a lot of people in the industry, so I've managed to find the best reporters to deal with. Trust me, when you're revealing your innermost thoughts and saucy sex secrets, it's important to be selling your soul to somebody you're comfortable with.

If you're really nervous, you can approach a news agency (no, not the place that sells lottery tickets and alcohol to under-18's) as a go-between. The pro is that they will negotiate a better fee, as the newspapers know they can't rip off a well-established agency; on the other hand, they will take a fee for doing nothing more than setting up the deal.

Better the Devil You Know – Which Newspaper?

The obvious choice for your debut kiss-and-tell splash is the *News of the World*. It's renowned for paying the highest fees and has the most prestige. They also have the best lawyers to fight those pesky injunctions footballers think they can put on any story. (Don't worry, we'll come to those later.)

The People is a great Sunday paper which, due to a feminist-leaning editor, has some really sympathetic kiss-and-tell stories. No sleaze here, thank you very much!

I did my first (and hopefully only) kiss-and-tell in *The People*, and it made what was essentially a very distressing time into what could be described as fun ... almost. They really were on my side, and didn't take the typical approach of 'Rich Footballer Shags Silly Girl'. Even when Wesley tried to put an injunction on them, they still went ahead. I was on the front page the very next day with the screaming headline, 'GAGGED!'*

The story focused on what this mystery footballer was getting away with, not so much on what size my bra was or what positions I most enjoyed. Newspapers often want to squeeze everything out of you, and there are certain things which only Wesley and I know that could have brought him public shame. I decided not to do this, and to stick with my decision not to name him. It wasn't so much a kiss-and-tell as a kiss-and-guess-who! So thank you, *The People*, for not giving up on me. They proved that not all newspapers are about shame and sleaze; sometimes they really do just want to tell the truth without feeling the need to ruin someone's life.

The Sport and *The Star* aren't typically associated with breaking kiss-and-tells, as their funds aren't as extensive as some of the other papers. They're more appropriate for

* Not gimp-style, just metaphorically speaking.

follow-up press, if you don't mind being a little bit salacious and getting your boobs out. (I've actually done a few little feature pieces for *The Star* over the years, and they have to be one of the nicest, easiest papers to work with.)

Not only should you feel comfortable with the newspaper, but also the journalist who you will be dealing with. Unfortunately that tabloid-journalist stereotype has, in my experience, turned out to be rather accurate. They will be your best friend one minute, trying to get you to say things you don't want to say and do things you don't want to do. Then, as soon as they have what they want, they're off without a trace.

Nor do many have the right determination or perceptiveness to really make the stories work. I tend to stay in touch with the same small number of writers, but I've now gathered quite a collection of contacts from newspapers, magazines and TV channels. Just yesterday, I was thinking of ways to drum up some publicity for *WAG Don't-Wannabe* when an email popped up in my inbox, telling me a book I had ordered through Tesco Books was delayed even further. (It's the follow-up to *Vice – 10 Years of Fashion Dos and Don'ts*. If you haven't read it, go get yourself a copy – it's hilarious!)

Instead of just deleting it I had a great idea. (*Ding!* That was the sound of a light-bulb going on in my head.) I decided to send a round robin email out to my bunch of journos, telling them how I had bought a book online over a year ago and how its publication date kept being put further and further back. I now wasn't due to receive it until November, almost a year and a half from when I ordered it! My little angle would be that, whilst I've been waiting for that book, I've written my own, got a publishing deal and publication date *before* I've even received the *Vice* book.

Straightaway one guy, who always seemed more interested in asking me out than writing a story, bluntly told me that it would never work. Funny that, as immediately after I received a contract from a women's weekly offering £200 for the story – it was only a fun piece, you see – and then an hour later a respected national daily asked me to sign an exclusive deal for an article on why I'm writing my book and what I want to achieve. (All for a fee, of course.)

I was more excited about the prospect of all the free publicity than I was the money – but that helps too! It just goes to show that you can find an angle and make an interesting story out of almost anything.

Now that's what I call a positive attitude – and a good morning's work.

But while some journalists lack enthusiasm, others can be plain nasty and devious. I once agreed to do an article with *The Sun* and the journalist, R, couldn't have been nicer – agreeing with me on a certain angle and promising my role would be to give advice to girls on dating footballers. (Namely, don't do it!)

We had agreed on copy and image approval and the deal was done. Then, as soon as she had what she wanted, she did a disappearing act, not returning emails or phone calls. Now I know why. The day before my 23rd birthday a two-page spread appeared with a headline and copy describing me as 'desperate', 'sordid' and 'vile', among other things. I hadn't been notified of its imminent publication, which seriously pissed off *Grazia* who had printed a story on me that very same day.

Grazia's story was 100 percent accurate, but if you read both pieces you wouldn't believe they were about the same girl. I wrote to the Press Complaints Commission and managed to have the story taken off of the internet, but not before several other gossip sites had claimed it as their own. (More of this later. See 'Public Perception and Bad Press'.)

Negotiating a Deal

"A verbal contract isn't worth the paper it's written on."
– Samuel Goldwyn, Hollywood mogul

Before you start *anything* it's important to strike a deal. While everything they want remains in your head and on your person your price is higher. It's *you* that's in control!

Most tabloid papers will agree a standard price with you, say about £10,000. They will then add to your contract that if it makes the front page it will go up to £15,000 and that if it's after page 25, in the back of the paper, it will only be £5,000 or something. Don't agree to this! There's no guarantee where in the paper the story will appear, and I've sometimes seen quite big stories in the middle somewhere.

They may try and sway you with the top-end price for the

front page, but unless you strike lucky – as I did, when it was a slow news day and footballers-behaving-badly scandals were a hot topic – then it's not likely you'll get it. Even if your guy is really high-profile there's no guarantee that, on the day before it's due to come out, some old-time celebrity won't die or a royal won't do something naughty. It's not worth the risk.

So try and even out the deal so that you know exactly what you're getting. And remember – don't let them lowball you. Once you've agreed to that first price you can't go back.

If, like me, you hate discussing money then there are better ways of doing it. These journos are old hands at this game.

When you're sitting across the table from someone with a contract in their hands and a specified amount already typed up, it can be hard to fight your corner. One way around this is to agree a price via email before meeting up. I don't even like discussing money on the telephone, but in an email I can put across exactly what I want to say with the confidence to ask for what I believe I deserve. (Maybe that's just because I've always felt more comfortable writing to somebody rather than talking to them face-to-face, if it's likely to get confrontational.) Name the price you want and explain why you think it's worth that much – make your point confidently and they will agree.

Remember, if you're smart, the price you get for your kiss-and-tell is just the starting point. Afterwards you can sell it on to other newspapers and women's glossy monthlies, then the lad's mags, then the celeb weeklies. I was also asked to be a guest on *Richard and Judy* and to be interviewed for BBC radio. Money can't buy you happiness, but it does bring you a more pleasant form of misery, as Spike Milligan once said.

Money isn't the only deciding factor, however. It's important to realise that a high-profile kiss-and-tell could potentially make you a lot of enemies, attract you a few stalkers and strain your existing relationships with the people around you – so it's imperative that you try to get the story as close to how you want to tell it as possible.

Of course, at the end of the day it's a Sunday tabloid and they're always going to want a bit of scandal, some sexy 'confessions' and revealing pictures – but there's a lot you can do to control this.

Ask for COPY APPROVAL and IMAGE APPROVAL. Copy approval is vital – while these journalists are acting so lovely towards you and bending over backwards to help you, that's because you have what they want. They're after a scandalous splash for Sunday, so it's up to you to make sure that the odd word here and there is removed or tweaked so that you come off a whole lot better.

"I felt helpless because the way The Sun *has written the piece was so clever and everyone would believe what they said. I also felt helpless at not being able to do anything about it."* – Cassie Sumner

When I agreed to do the piece for *The Sun*, it was actually supposed to be about this book. I was going to be their 'expert' on the seedy world of footballers. (What a distinction to hold!) But they just turned all the information I gave them back on me, as if I was the one who was responsible for it all. It made me look terrible.

I'm sure you'll see I'm not being oversensitive when I list some more of the words they used to describe me: 'depraved', 'pathetic', 'promiscuous' ... you'd think they were describing a paedophile or a rapist, not a young club girl idealistic enough to try to put the world of the Premiership to rights at the age of 22.

If you're exposing their precious football stars you will always be the enemy, no matter how good your intentions are. The moral of the story is to always have your copy approval set in stone. (Or written in blood!)

Image approval is always a handy little thing to have, although slightly more difficult to obtain. After all, if millions of people are going to see you in your underwear (or less) in a national newspaper, you want it to be a *good* picture. I'm not saying that the people who deal with the images aren't good at their jobs, but they just won't care as much as you do.

One of the Sunday newspapers' kiss-and-tells on Jermain Defoe (and who hasn't done a kiss-and-tell on Jermain?) was based around how much he loved the girl's huge breasts. This would have been fine, if it wasn't for the fact that she was leaning over in the picture with a big chicken fillet hanging out of her bra! The poor girl must have been absolutely mortified. I still don't understand how it got past the photographer, who had taken hundreds of pictures, the stylist on the shoot, the journalist who put the final piece together, the editor who checked it, the proof reader … The point is, trust no one. Only trust yourself – and check everything yourself!

When a photographer has taken so many pictures there are always going to be one or two where you're gurning slightly from smiling for hours, or squinting a bit from staring at the bright studio lights – and you can guarantee that they will pick the one where you're both gurning and squinting, and maybe looking a bit fatter than you really are. Only you have the power to stop this – get image approval!

I remember one time I did a photo shoot for a national newspaper and the story went in without my knowing, so I didn't get image approval. I was happy enough with the picture – it wasn't the best, but there was nothing hideously wrong with it either. The photographer kindly emailed me lots of the pictures he took a couple of days later, and I could easily pick out five pictures that were 100 percent better than the one they featured.

And speaking of pictures, let's get onto the shoot itself.

Flashing Lights & Photo Shoots

Press photo shoots are often well done, with top makeup artists, hair stylists and photographers on hand. Remember though, newspapers will very, very rarely airbrush any pictures and so I always like to prepare well for a shoot if given enough warning by doing the following:

One week before: Stop all steam rooms and saunas – these break out your skin in spots, the last thing you need! Also, if you have your hair regularly highlighted or coloured, get it done now! Those pesky photographers don't bother to airbrush out your roots. For what could be done in a few clicks of a mouse, you have to spend hours in a salon chair. Grrr ...

Four days before: Buy some organic, un-waxed lemons, squeeze them into hot water and drink through a straw (to protect your teeth from the acid) all day. This has an amazing effect on your body in the short term. You skin will be clear and glowing, with all signs of bloating gone, and you'll feel on top of the world! Even if you're given a photo shoot at the last minute, it's always worth doing this for as little as half a day – it just perks up your skin a treat, and makes you look and feel like a million dollars. I even do it before a big party, or any other time I want to look my best.

Two days before: Exfoliate your entire body, including your face. Get rid of all that old, dead skin and your young, glowing skin will really shine through in the pictures. Of course, you can always fake this last minute-stylee with some Shimmery body lotion.

One day before: Give your hair a hot oil treatment, or a deep conditioner, and leave on while you're relaxing in the bath or spa. The light steam will open up the hairs and the treatment will work amazingly! Also make sure all your waxing is done well in advance. Pluck your eyebrows so they're freshly done.

On the day: Cleanse and moisturise carefully and go to the shoot with a bare face. The makeup artists rarely bother taking off your previous layer and it can really affect the final result. I once did a photo shoot for a top glossy weekly magazine and, by the time they came to do my makeup, they just put a completely different coloured foundation over the one I had on, and all my old powder. The result was messy, and I still can't bring myself to look at those pictures!

Blow-dry your hair carefully and be sure not to style it too rigidly. The hairstylist will do all that on the day.

Smother yourself in a slightly Shimmery (not glittery) body lotion and, if you're really in need, add a touch of Sun Shimmer to give your sun-starved skin a bit of colour if it's the middle of winter. A little bit of Sun Shimmer goes a long way when you're naked in front of a camera!

Although there will be a stylist with cases full of clothes on the shoot, it's always wise to take some of your own things. I really don't know why they bother paying stylists when you end up almost naked anyway. On two big shoots I've done for national newspapers I've ended up wearing a pair of my own black knickers, which were part of a set in Primark for about £6! I don't know what it is about those pants, but photographers love them!

As a general rule it's always good to take:

- Basic knickers which really suit you, in either black or white. These are often used, and it's a case of the simpler the better.
- Any lingerie sets you have that are striking and revealing.

- A good corset. This is a great alternative if you're not mad about your stomach.

- Any shoes that you really love. The stylist's shoes won't always fit you and you may have Louboutin or Gina when she only has New Look.

- Anything you feel comfortable in. They might say the shoot will start with you wearing a sexy evening dress, then graduate onto underwear, then sometimes implied (or actual) topless-ness. But I will virtually guarantee they'll use the most revealing ones, so I wouldn't worry about the dress!

- Definitely take some of your own makeup. I always find that if I don't like the way they've done it, I usually want to add a little more blusher or bronzer. Excuse yourself to go to the bathroom, take your bag with you (with your make up sneakily snuggled inside) and get to work! Don't worry if your face begins to resemble Coco the Clown both in character and colour – the camera requires at least three times the normal amount of makeup for it to show up. The only person who may notice that you've added your own finishing touches is the makeup artist herself, and she won't say anything.

Also make sure you take a selection of your own jewellery as the stylist doesn't always have this, especially not earrings. Take dramatic stuff like huge, chunky beads, dangly, jewel-laden earrings and quirky rings. It will all look great in the shots if you're really feeling comfortable with the photographer and stylist. I have some chunky bracelets in bright candy colours like pink and yellow, and if I'm wearing matching or contrasting underwear it can look great. If you're not so sure then just start by wearing a cute pair of diamond studs which go with everything and a pretty ring or bracelet, and suggest the crazy stuff later.

It's always good to have one signature piece that you wear pretty much all of the time. Mine is a beautiful ring which my next-door neighbour made in India. She spends half the year there, buying materials to make these stunning rings. They're all one-offs so I know that no one else will have one like mine. It's nice to have that little personal touch running through your press too, if you're planning on doing lots of it.

What to Expect at a Press Photo-Shoot

Sometimes when I go for a shoot, the makeup or hair person can be really, well, shit. But in my experience newspapers that deal in big stories use only the best people. So don't worry. Arrive with unstyled hair and no makeup to make it easier for all involved.

You will usually be introduced to the photographer and stylists, but not the many lighting staff or other staff. You'll then be taken into the makeup room, asked to take off all your clothes and to put a robe on. But don't worry, this isn't what your mum warned you about – it's so you don't have any unsightly clothes lines from your bra, socks, etc in the pictures.

Hair and makeup will begin their work. Don't be afraid to

ask for something specific, or to say if you don't like something. It's your face, your hair, and if you're not comfortable with it, it will show in the pictures. I used to ask to do my own eyeliner and mascara, as I just couldn't stand having someone with a wand that close to my vulnerable open eyeball! A good trick one makeup artist taught me, which helped to overcome this (quite natural) fear of sharp objects coming towards my open eye, is to look in the opposite direction of whatever is coming at me. For example, if someone is doing the upper outer corners of my eyelashes, then I look down toward my nose. It works every time!

If you're body-shy, now is the time to get over it. Stylists and makeup artists will not leave the room when they ask you to try on different underwear and outfits. This means that you need to get butt-naked in front of a roomful of people you just met. A bit like a night out at Chinawhite ...

The stylist will have lots of options for what you can wear. You'll probably start off in a cocktail dress to make you more comfortable, then they'll move you on to underwear, then at the end they'll probably say, "Let's do some implied topless." You may be recoiling in horror now, but when everyone's acting like it's the most normal thing in the world you will feel slightly pressured to do it. Trust me, it's these last ones that always make the paper.

In case you're confused, 'implied topless' or 'implied nude' is when you're either naked or topless but not actually showing anything. The grand mistress of this is Lucy Pinder, a glamour model famed for not showing everything. She's always topless in her pictures, but for the first three or four years of her career there was never any sign of a nipple. For all we knew she may not have had any. (Did anyone ever ask her?)

This is acceptable in a national newspaper. For my kiss-and-tell with *The People*, I only had on a pair of black knickers (yes, *those* ones again!) and my arms were up over my body, cupping my face. No one would see a thing!

The only problem was that photographers don't do *any* airbrushing of their feature pictures, and at that particular angle you could fully see the fresh scar under one of my boobs. This is exactly what I mean about not trusting photographers, picture editors, etc. Check everything yourself and get that essential image approval!

Clearly, at that time I wasn't listening to my own advice. Fool. We did the photo shoot about an hour before the paper went to print as we'd been caught up in a legal fight all day. Once again, I've made all these mistakes so that I can pass invaluable advice to you, dear reader.

The Interview (a.k.a. The 1001 Most Personal Questions about Your Sex Life)

It's time to get personal. When you agree to do a story with a particular paper, be prepared to divulge every secret you have. Things that you wouldn't tell your best friend, let alone your mum, are going to be revealed to the rest of the world. So be prepared for that!

Soon after first contact, a journalist will come and meet you to discuss the story and get you to sign a contract. This is just a confidentiality agreement which states the story is being sold exclusively to them, and that you can't go and talk to any other newspaper or magazine about it. It should also have the agreed sum for the story in there, along with the name of the footballer in question.

You should be 100 percent happy with the contract before signing it. From my experience, this is of paramount importance. When I signed my deal with the *News of the World*, I wasn't ready to end it with Wesley. I had regrets from the start and was still being controlled by my heart, not my head.

I remember one morning on the train into London, calling the journalist and begging him to stop the story. I would do anything if only we could stop it, and no one would find out about it. Then Wesley and I could continue to live happily ever after.

As if! Although, looking back, it seemed like a good thing that they stopped the story at the time, I felt like my heart was slowly being wrenched from my body and there was nothing I could do about it. The worst part of it was that I felt like it was entirely my fault.

Anyway, back to the interview. You should choose somewhere nice and quiet, as they may be using a dictaphone and it's less stressful if you can sit down somewhere discreet. I remember once, when I did a story, we had to sit on one of those bars in Starbucks that face out onto a busy street, where the people sitting next to you are almost on your lap. As I revealed more and more personal details, I could see the man next to me straining his ears and sneaking quick looks. Relaxing it was *not*.

I would also choose a lunchtime at work. This is for the simple reason that I use on first dates too – if you feel uncomfortable in the situation you can always use the excuse, "I have to get back to work now!" If you say beforehand that you only have an hour then you should be able to walk away after that time. If it's going badly and you're feeling out of control, you can escape. Even if it's going well you can get away and think properly about what's happened and go on from there.

Evidence: Exhibit A

> "He's a stranger to me now. The way he dealt with
> the whole thing. He's just a very different man."
> – Rebecca Loos

One of the main parts of the deal which will affect how much the story is worth is evidence. Cold, hard evidence. While your best friends might know that every word you tell them is the gospel, journalists don't – and you could just be dreaming this up to make a quick buck.

One of the most important things to remember is SAVE YOUR TEXT MESSAGES. Save every one you can, until your phone is at capacity, and the more salacious and incriminating they are the better. And watch out – some footballers have a second phone which is pay-as-you-go. You don't need to register these phones to a name or address, so they can be tricky for journalists to trace.

But when you're receiving messages every day for months on end, it can be hard to determine which ones are important to keep. When you have your interview with the newspaper, one of the first things they will do is photograph your phone and every single text message you have. As these are often downright dirty it can be hard to look the photographer in the eye after that.

(One of the reasons I'm considering setting up my own agency dealing with kiss-and-tells is because I know that being in a roomful of journalists and photographers, having to reveal every intimate detail of your love life and show private messages to strange men, can be very unnerving and lonely. As much as they're acting like they're your best friends, you can't help but think they're judging you.)

Picture messages are useful to keep too, and if you have a naked one where his face is visible you've hit the jackpot.

The paper may also ask you to call him or meet him while you're wired up, so that they can tape your conversation. I point-blank refused to do this – it was just going too far for me, and I definitely didn't hate Wesley enough. At that time I was feeling extremely pressured, and didn't want to give them any more information than they already had.

But if you really want revenge on somebody – why not?

Let me tell you a little tale, one of Francesca's Fables. It's a word of warning on why you should definitely keep all your text messages:

Back in the offices of *The People*, it was a Saturday and my story was due to come out on the following day. Time was of the essence, and the photo shoot had stopped to make way for a fight with his lawyers. They, along with Wesley, were battling to keep the situation under their control. Faxes were jumping back and forth between us, each getting more frantic than the last. I think Wesley realised that I meant business now, and that he couldn't buy my compliance with holidays or cars. So he eventually resorted to something which I can never forgive him for – even though it was probably his annoyingly patronising and pushy lawyer who took action.

They called the police out on *The People* and I. The POLICE! I'd never heard of anything like it! By now they had come up with the frankly startling story that, on the night of his infamous Christmas party (which I now like to call 'Tinselgate'), I, a weakling girl, had made a massive, muscular guy feel "scared for his life".

He also tried to get me done for extortion, saying that I had *made* him give me several thousand pounds. Luckily for me (and here's the moral of the story, girls), I had my backups. For what seems like the first time in this entire book, I'd listened to my own goddamned advice!

Swiftly, the journalists went through piles of papers on a desk which I soon realised were copies of my text messages. Problem number one was solved by:

WAG Don't-Wannabe

"My friends dragged me away, where are you? I will come and find you." – Wesley, by text.

*"Where can I f*** you when I get up?"* *
– Wesley, by text.

*"I will come and f*** you if you have somewhere."*
– Wesley, by text.

They were all sent within an hour of the alleged 'attack'. Now I'm not a detective, but I'm pretty sure that a 'victim' doesn't send messages like that to his 'attacker' less than an hour after the incident. Maybe I got inside his head and forced him to send them with my super-intimidating skills? (I wouldn't have been surprised if they'd come back with that one next.)

Needless to say, the texts were sent straight over and they were forced to drop that issue immediately. I would love to have been a fly on the wall in their office at that time!

The next issue to deal with was the alleged extortion. Once more, I flipped through the papers and soon found:

"Hi babe, hope you're ok, can you send me your bank details pls it's only fair" – Wesley, by text.

"I owe you one. What do you want? Anything."
– Wesley, by text.

* *How romantic!*

171

"You sure you don't want anything? You okay and do you want to go away somewhere? For as long as you like. Take your friends." – Wesley, by text.

As you can see, they all proved that he kept trying to give me money and holidays, but I had turned them all down. He even had to resort to begging me to give him my bank details, so I was hardly holding him upside down and shaking his pockets out. Extortion, my arse!

The smug satisfaction of knowing I could prove him wrong again was fabulous! Although it had got me off the hook, however, it was bittersweet, as it soon dawned on me that he had made serious allegations that were completely fabricated, regardless of any repercussions for me. Thank goodness I'm smart enough (or maybe cynical enough) to keep my messages. But what if I hadn't? Who knows what could have happened to me?

What a bastard.

That's the great thing about being blonde. People think you're as dumb as they are, and when I want to I can pull it off quite well. It's not easy acting dumb – but it's certainly helped me!

ALLY MCBEAL IT ISN'T –
DEALING WITH LAWYERS

*"Weasling out of things is important to learn. It's what
separates us from the animals ... except the weasel."*
– Homer Simpson

"I did not have sexual relations with that woman."
– Bill Clinton

This brings me neatly on to the subject of lawyers. Now trust
me, girls, there is plenty I would love to say here but for fear
of reprisals I have to really watch myself. Quite often, the evil
that footballers do is done via their lawyers or agents. (Oh,
didn't you know that? Footballers don't tend to make
decisions for themselves. Why, when you can pay someone
else to think for you?)

I believe lawyers are the root of all evil where footballers
are concerned. Being at their disposal night and day is what

has made them so blasé about their lifestyle and sleeping habits. One call away is a top lawyer who will be willing to stay up all night, working around the clock to make sure that no one finds out the dirty little secrets. Sign a cheque and the problem is gone in a puff of smoke. In the world of footballers, anything can be made to disappear – including *you*, and any 'relationship' you may have had.

After Amelia went to the *News of the World* and I got caught up in it all, Wesley found out. I'd met him the day before in an attempt to somehow tell him about the mess I'd gotten into, but I just couldn't. For once I didn't know best, and I couldn't sort it out on my own.

When he found out he went mad (understandably), and wanted to meet me for lunch the next day to talk about it. Come lunchtime, I warned my receptionist friend at the office that I may be a little late as I had a tiny problem to sort out. What an understatement! I ended up being taken to a solicitor's office for nine hours. (Did you get that? NINE HOURS!)

Let me tell you what happened …

I went outside to meet him at the agreed place, my office building. I was on the phone to him when I suddenly saw his car, a black Bentley-type thing. As I started to walk towards him, the strangest thing happened – he told me not to get in his car but to look to my right and get in another car instead. A huge, blacked-out Range Rover sat there with a menacing driver staring straight at me.

I wanted to turn and run but I was made to get inside.

Once I was in, the driver centrally locked the doors and drove off at an alarming rate. I don't know what he thought I was going to do. Jump out of a moving vehicle onto a busy Cannon Street?

I repeatedly asked the driver – who looked like an extra from *Crimewatch* – where we were going. Silence. "How long is it going to take to get there?" Silence. "Who are you?" Finally he answered. "I'm employed to drive you. I cannot tell you where we're going."

I started to freak out. I genuinely thought they were going to get rid of me. It's not that crazy when you think about it – people hire hitmen all the time in this country, and if common thugs with a grudge can do it, what's to stop a multimillionaire footballer doing it to protect his precious reputation?

This is it, I thought as we sped through the streets of London into unfamiliar territory. *I am going to die. I bet there's a shovel in the boot and a freshly dug hole in Epping Forest with my name on it.* (Not literally, of course. Footballers are dumb, but hitmen probably aren't quite as silly.)

We eventually pulled up to a gated entrance which led to an area at the back of a large building. I asked where we were. Instead of answering me, the driver just got out and met a stern looking woman in a suit. They talked in hushed voices (at least they sounded hushed through the thick tinted glass), stole glances in my direction and nodded.

I couldn't help wondering whether they were agreeing to

stab me or shoot me. Or to bury me like Saskia in *Eastenders*, or just throw me in the Thames gangster-style. Maybe it was going to be like *Saw*, and they were going to put me through some horribly dangerous trial with potentially fatal results to make me 'learn my lesson'.

This wasn't how I'd imagined my lunch with Wesley was going to be, in all honesty, and I called my friend Andrea in a panic. She told me not to worry; if she didn't hear from me by six she would call the police. (She didn't, actually. By the time I was released it was 9:00pm, and she was in the process of getting drunk in one of the City's many suit-filled watering holes.)

I was eventually taken out of the car (thank goodness – I was starting to feel like one of those dogs you see trapped in hot cars, licking the windows) and into a boardroom with several people facing me. Uh-oh. These, I was informed, were Wesley's team of lawyers – that's right, a whole *team*. His main man, who for the purposes of this book I shall call Patronising Pete, was caught up in traffic and would be with us in about two hours. (By which time I was supposed to be back at work, dammit!)

The stern looking woman didn't look so stern once we were inside, more disapproving. It was like when you were caught doing something really naughty and your mum wasn't angry, just disappointed, which is so much worse …

As I sat down I felt that dreaded feeling. There are times when I just really want to be strong, to be able to hold my ground and not be such a … such a *girl*! But as I began to speak I started to cry, out of anger and sadness as the enormity of what had happened dawned on me. She offered me a tissue, and some advice. "Just be honest with us, Wesley wants to help both of you."

Which was bollocks! Wesley was only out for himself.

I hated myself for being so vulnerable. Lawyers pick up on the slightest weakness and exploit it, and here I was laying myself open to the enemy. Just as I was explaining how I'd been taken from my office and brought there like a captured fugitive, in walked Wesley, looking annoyingly hot.

Double damn! Now it looked like I was sitting there crying in a room full of solicitors because I'd been caught out. Nothing could have been further from the truth. Before I knew what I was doing, I broke from tears to rage. "How dare you bring me here like this?" I shouted at him. "You've technically kidnapped me and that is ILLEGAL!" I pointed out helpfully. He immediately apologised and looked like he actually meant it. The solicitors told me they didn't know how I'd been brought there, and agreed that it was very wrong. Naughty Wesley.

We sat and talked it out for several hours. Each word was painful and strained. Here I was, sitting with a roomful of legal eagles and the one man I didn't want inconvenienced by this whole mess, trying to defend myself. Several times he asked them all to leave the room so we could speak alone, and I think he believed what I was saying, which was all I could ask for. We agreed to work together and to stop the story, thereby protecting everyone involved. Wesley promised that he would try to see me more; although he and his girlfriend were together now, who knew what was going to happen in the future?

I was being won over, and he could tell. If I could go back in time and give myself a massive flick on the forehead to wake myself up, I would. What a fool I was being.

By the time Patronising Pete arrived, the whole team and Wesley knew the facts surrounding the story. I was not to blame, I wanted it to stop, and I still wanted to see Wesley. (FOOL!)

Then PP swept in with an air of self-importance and stated who he was. I had heard of him and groaned inwardly. *Here we go,* I thought, *I may as well go and jump into that hole in Epping Forest myself.* He started telling me all about Wesley and his delicate situation at home, and how I was the key that could make it all better. He talked to me like a fricking retard for over twenty minutes, and I felt myself getting angrier and angrier. When he finally finished his speech with, "So let's get this silly little misunderstanding out of the way and sign this, eh sweetheart?" I exploded. How dare he talk to me like I was some mentally retarded gold-digger?!

I told him exactly how I felt. I could see right through his silly little charade of 'working together', getting me to sign a false statement saying I'd made the whole thing up, that the newspaper had practically held me at gunpoint and I didn't want it to go to press. Although that morning I'd have given anything to turn back the clock, I now felt an overwhelming desire to defy this man and everyone else in the room who thought they could just buy me with sweet talk and good old-fashioned cash.

In a move which went against everything I'd said previously and completely amazed Wesley, I refused point-blank to sign the damned thing. I was standing up for myself for the first time that day. I'd been duped, kidnapped and questioned for hours like some kind of criminal – and all I was offered in return was a quick getaway if I signed. Well, they weren't getting me that easily.

I demanded my own solicitor – not Dave from down the hall, but an independent one. He arrived and we went into a separate room to discuss the case. I told him *almost* everything, as I've learnt never to show all your cards, not even to your lawyer. I was right too. This so-called 'independent' solicitor was actually a good friend of Patronising Pete and they went to the Bahamas every winter together. That's the thing about solicitors – they'll look you in the eye whilst they fuck you in the arse.

I felt enraged with Wesley and his team, and told my solicitor (who we shall call Martin) that I wasn't just going to bow down to whatever they wanted. I tried to explain (as much as a weepy girl can explain to a suited, booted, stern lawyer) that I had really fallen for him and that they wanted me to wipe away six months of my life with one signature. It wasn't fair. I was determined not to back down.

Martin and Patronising Pete exchanged words every half an hour or so over the next couple of hours, and would often disappear for 'talks' for a good twenty minutes. I personally think they were in the back office just knocking back shots or having 40 winks to get them through this charade, but of course I'll never know.

During one of these times I asked Martin if Wesley could come in and sit with me. A few minutes later Wesley walked in and sat beside me, so close yet so far away. It seemed wrong to even touch, when touching each other was the very reason we were here! I asked him if he minded that I'd asked him to come in, and he looked confused.

Obviously a footballer looks confused most of the time, but this was different. He said he'd just told Pete that he wanted to come in and talk to me, and that Martin hadn't said a thing. How weird is that? The part of me that wanted to believe, more than anything, that we were meant to be together was suddenly flooded with thoughts of Mystic Meg-style destiny.

Maybe it was their tactic to have him come and talk to me. My heart had melted just a little, and I knew then that I would do what he wanted. I wanted to believe so badly that we could carry on, I'd have done anything just to make him happy. It seems odd, in retrospect, given that what he wanted me to do was to save his primary relationship – but that irony was lost on me at the time.

Martin came back and we moved on to his offices around the corner. By this time it was 7:00pm and I'd been there for just over seven hours. The stress of the day, not to mention the lack of food, had brought on the most severe migraine I've known. I suffer from migraine quite badly and had been hospitalised for it several times before then. Earlier that day, when it had started to get bad, I'd asked for painkillers and had taken about six as I didn't think they would touch my pain. Nobody stopped me – I could have killed myself!

By now I was at the stage of severe migraine + no food + six painkillers rolling around my empty stomach, and I felt like I'd downed about ten sambuca shots. Slurring and stumbling, I rattled out my order of events to my solicitor from my upside-down position on a squishy old sofa, whilst he typed as slow as a one-fingered racoon on a laptop.

I must have looked like an absolute nutcase junkie, but that's just what I get like when I have a really bad attack. He asked me to eat something as he thought I was going to keel over, and sent a colleague out to get me a hot chocolate and crisps from the local Starbucks. When said boy came back with a blueberry muffin I freaked out.

"I can't eat this! I am ALLERGIC to blueberries. [I'm not.] Do you want me to DIE? Is that what you want? Probably then we can all go HOME!" I shouted/slurred, and then promptly began to eat the muffin.

(Wow! I'd never had one before – it was good!)

"*STOOOOOOP!*" they yelled. "You're allergic!"

"Aahh, that's okay," I slurred as I proceeded to eat it up like some kind of culinary Evel Knievel. What a diva! What a bitch!

To be fair to me, I'd had enough by then. It was getting on for 9:00pm and no one at my office even knew where I was. I had been questioned and cross-examined for nine hours and I just wanted to go home. It's funny how the solicitors went on about the journalists railroading me into signing things I wasn't happy to sign, and here they were doing it to me again! Someone thrust a piece of paper in front of me and a pen into my hand and I just signed away. I didn't even care by then.

This is what it said. It's a rare glimpse of what goes on behind the headlines, and it's typical of the situation a girl like me can find herself in:

IN THE HIGH COURT OF JUSTICE
QUEENS BENCH DIVISION
BETWEEN:

FRANCESCA AMBER SAWYER (Claimant)
[*Claimant? I never* claimed *anything, did I?*]
And
************* (Defendant)

WITNESS STATEMENT OF FRANCESCA
AMBER SAWYER

I, FRANCESCA AMBER SAWYER c/o ****** *******
Solicitors and Advocates , *** ****** ******** London
**** *** will say as follows:

1. I am a personal assistant working for a private commodities investment company in the City of London. I am 22 years old. My mother has ME and suffers with high blood pressure.

WAG Don't-Wannabe

[What the frick has that got to do with the price of cheese? I don't know where they got my mum's medical information from, I really don't.]

2. I have been involved in a relationship with ******
   ********** since June 2007. We were not seen in public
   together as a couple and took steps to keep the
   relationship secret. We met in private. A few weeks ago, I
   was approached by a journalist, named ******, asking
   me questions about ******. I believe that a friend of
   mine had found out about the relationship.

*[What BS. Never in public together? How about the night
we met? What about the club's Christmas party?* *]*

3. He said that the *News of the World* newspaper was
   going to run a story about our relationship. I was told
   that the story would be published whether or not I co-
   operated. He said that if I co-operated, the story would
   be less dramatic and I would be portrayed as the
   innocent party. I was worried about the effect of a story
   on my mother and my employers. The *News of the
   World* has a massive amount of readers ... I was not
   happy about the situation generally ...

*[Oh, they're the ones who are being dramatic here. What's
all this about my mother again too? They're obsessed*

---

* *Why didn't Wesley and I almost fornicating in the middle of a west London nightclub count? Oh yes, those tricky little men at the football club ensured the entire club was on 'private hire', thus making it – you got it – a private place! WTF? So anything that happened there took place on private premises and therefore doesn't count. Clever, eh?*

with her, just like a nutter was once after she was on the Vanessa *show. 'Local Celebrity Was My Mum' – for a fortnight at least.*]

4. I was told I must decide quickly. I agreed to meet journalists from the *News of the World*. I was given a contributor's agreement and asked to sign it. At the time I felt that I did not have any alternative. I did not seek any legal advice at the time … I signed the document, letting the situation become tomorrow's problem and went along with what the newspaper asked including having photographs taken. I was not given a copy of the agreement that I signed.

[*The pictures were really darn good as well, though they never got to see print. Most amazing makeup artist too – want her for my wedding.*]

5. One morning after I signed the agreement I had second thoughts after speaking to ****** (he did not know about the story at the time) and called ********. He said that if I did not go along with it, the *News of the World* would get nasty and do it anyway.

6. Today was the first time that I obtained legal advice and realised that I might be able to stop the story. ****** has now found out about it and I now realise just how damaging it would be for him.

[*'Obtained legal advice' makes it sound like I just strolled*

into my local Citizen's Advice Bureau, rather than getting
kidnapped and driven at high speed to a secret location for
nine hours! Talk about selective wording ...]

7. I do not want the story to be published. I have always
   been concerned about the effect of a story on me, but felt
   that there was nothing that I could do to stop it. It
   would cause both me and my mother serious distress and
   embarrassment. In addition, I believe it would have a
   negative impact on my career.

8. My sister works for a PR company. Through her, I have
   been interviewed voluntarily for feature articles in
   magazines and some newspapers. In the course of these
   interviews I have talked about relationships, but I have
   never disclosed the identity of a boyfriend or talked in
   any detail about sexual relationships. I draw a distinction
   between material like this and a long article in the *News
   of the World* going into detail about a relationship that I
   have tried to keep private.

[*Shit! Looks like my media-whoreness came back to haunt
me. Who knew they would Google me? That's just cruel!*]

9. I believe that the facts in this witness statement are true.
[*For which read: I believe I am as high as a kite
flying through Amsterdam right now, and this statement
I'm signing could say I want gender reassignment,
for all I know.*]

I have to stress the severity of my migraines at this point. I read a study where a person's condition during an attack was classed as one of the most debilitating known to medical science, and during that time I was being cross-examined and asked to sign legal statements.

With hindsight I can see that was a really bad situation to put me in, and I feel quite angry about that. Maybe I wouldn't have said what I said, did what I did, signed what I signed (or even eaten what I ate) if I was in the right state of mind. Was I temporarily insane? I think that, under those circumstances, the witness statement I signed shouldn't even be valid.

I finally got home at about 11:00pm, despite being told to stay in a London hotel for the foreseeable future and then go abroad somewhere for about a month after that.

I just sat down and cried. For all the wasted months I'd spent with Wesley; for what this meant for my future; for letting my employers down, letting myself down, and because I was mentally exhausted and looked like shit on a stick. I took more tablets and fell asleep next to my little dog, hoping that everything would be different in the morning.

All that weekend my friend Andrea tried to stop me thinking about it. The lawyers had told me that if I wasn't going to go into a hotel and cut off my phone, then I should keep myself busy for this weekend at least. I don't know if they were worried that the newspapers were going to try and contact me again (they did), or if I was going to try to kill myself (I didn't) – but I agreed for the sake of my sanity.

Wesley called several times to check that I was okay, and I couldn't help wondering why he hadn't been so attentive before. After all, it wasn't as if he couldn't have stayed in touch with me more.

I tried to not let it wind me up, and I was surprised at how nice he was being about the whole thing. The solicitors had told us the day before that they had never had a case like this, where the two people involved were even speaking, let alone wanting to be alone in the same room together and calling each other afterwards.

So maybe there was hope.

Maybe I'm being a little melodramatic but it really was a harrowing experience – for both of us, I guess. Wesley was particularly down at that time, what with his close family member's death and problems with the girlfriend. I found out via the ******** newspaper a month later that she had already temporarily moved out by this point!

When he had tried to tell me that he had some 'news' before, I'd thought he was going to say she was pregnant and I didn't want to know.

That's when it started, right there in the middle of Primark. As I was talking to him on the phone it was like an epiphany, as if all the previous months of lies and deceit were finally making sense to me – making me see this 'relationship' for what it was. A sham.

Over the next couple of weeks he became more and more distant, and I realised that he just wanted me to be what I had always been – his dirty little secret, his secret mistress locked away in the Love Shack, brought out on special occasions to entertain him with my sexy underwear and an adoring look in my eyes. I wasn't there to give him hassle about us seeing each other more, or why he should cheer me up when I was having a bad day. We were on dangerous middle ground. It was more than a casual fling, yet it would never be what I now desperately wanted it to become.

"Hell hath no fury like a woman scorned."

The last straw for me had been Wesley's football club's Christmas party, which I attended in December 2007. I realised then I just couldn't go on living my life like this – half normal, half secret; locked in a torrid affair with feelings that weren't getting any weaker with time, only stronger. It was like being in a time warp, and I was a pathetic pre-feminism housewife – only without the house or the wife part. I suddenly saw how he'd lavished most attention on me when he thought I was going to spill the beans. As soon as I could see how they had coaxed me into doing exactly what they wanted, I wasn't just angry. I was *furious*.

I could see that this well-oiled machine (I'm talking about the whole process, not Wesley!) had been used on girls like me time and time again. Not only had I had many predecessors, but many girls would unwittingly follow me like lambs to the slaughter. This is when the concept of *WAG Don't-Wannabe* was born.

I decided, after sharing half a bottle of vodka and half a

pint of tears with my trusty friend Andrea, that I would not let this beat me. I was going to have revenge my way. Kiss and tell? Shut up, I'm not that predictable …

I went straight to my favourite tabloid and told them I had a story that runs deeper than simply naming and shaming. *The People* is a Sunday, of course, so if you needed to know how I was duped into a relationship with a married man, you also needed to know my bra size and to see a picture of me in my knickers.

I'm proud to say that it made front-page news.

I then went on to start my own little campaign to expose exactly what happens in the seedy world of the Premiership. It saw me on the sofa at *Richard and Judy*'s, on a double-page spread in *The Sun*, debating with Ian Wright's ex-wife in a glossy, and giving my opinion in *Grazia*. It seemed that everyone was interested in what I had to say, and I took that as good news.

But as I soon learned, not all publicity is good publicity …

PUBLIC PERCEPTION
AND BAD PRESS

*"I'm not sure I want popular opinion on my side –
I've noticed those with the most opinions often have
the fewest facts."* – Bethania McKenstry

It's very easy for the general public, journalists, judgemental 'celebrity' columnists or anyone else to accuse kiss-and-tell girls of being 'trash' or 'gold diggers'. Unfortunately, in this country a lot of journalists – as well as a whole load of blog-tards who set up stupid gossip websites – tend to take this easy, predictable route. Seek out the right people and you may just get your point across in the right way. However, there's still a lot of progress to be made as to how footballers' girlfriends are perceived, as far as I'm concerned.

I remember, when I was younger, I'd read the *News of the World* on a Sunday and listen to my mum exclaim how the kiss-and-tell girls were 'shameless' or were 'degrading themselves'. Maybe I'm wired wrong, but I just can't see it. Especially now that, having been through the process myself, I can see how potentially liberating it is, and how it offers opportunities in the most unlikely of places.

Revenge Is a Dish Best Served on the Front Page

It's not all about the press and the money though, believe it or not. People forget the classic motivation for kiss and tell – SWEET REVENGE. Once I was well and truly tied into doing the story on Wesley, I got stuck in good and proper. I wanted to hurt him, and to show him how much he had hurt me.

Since then, as research for this book, I've been involved with the odd footballer or three and I've not felt even the slightest desire to piss them off by selling out their dirty secrets. I'm clearly not as much of a mercenary media-whore as I first thought! What I'm saying is that, for some women, and most definitely for me, it's often anger and revenge that makes them sell their story – *not* money.

Of course, not all stories are this way. Nowadays, in our throwaway celebrity culture, lots of kiss-and-tells are put together as mechanically as:

Wednesday: Shag a celeb in Chinawhite. Thursday: Ring the *News of the Screws*. Friday: Sell my sordid secrets and get baps out for pictures. Sunday: *Ta da!* £15k please!

But read between the lines of the heavily edited, partly glorified tales and you will sometimes, just sometimes, see the genuine heartache and misery behind it.

WAG Don't-Wannabe

Public perception is definitely swayed by how the piece is written. Sometimes people can be just plain nasty because you're a young woman doing what you want to do. I once had a piece published in my local newspaper back in Essex, *The Echo*; apart from the fact they called me an 'ex-WAG', they put across my story in a really positive way. I'll let you read it for yourself:

"Francesca Amber Sawyer, 22, from Canvey … is warning girls about the dangers of being a footballer's wife or girlfriend, known as a WAG, in a new book that she hopes will give useful guidelines on what to do when your other half is a soccer star …

"She said: 'I've been a regular on the London party circuit for about two years and, in that time, dated footballers. I didn't even know they were footballers to begin with.

"'The second guy, who played for England, I broke up with just before Christmas. We had a seven-month relationship. It ended badly and I got really hurt …

"'I don't regret my time with footballers. I've been to some amazing places I never would otherwise have had a chance to see, and do things I never would have got to do.

"'I've been flown out to private parties all over the world. Just last summer I was taken out to St Tropez for a P Diddy party. It was crazy!'

"But Francesca has now turned her back on dating footballers and hopes to publish her book within twelve months …"

Great, I thought, it mentions the book, I don't sound too dumb and they didn't misquote me or try to trip me up. At last – a perfectly positive piece! I couldn't have been happier. For the first time in ages I actually told my grandparents and all my friends to read it. Although they all thought it was great, however, not everybody did.

Unfortunately, when I checked on the newspaper's website the next day, there were some very unsavoury comments about me posted there. (I say 'some' – there were lots! More than 100.) These were mostly from people who had never even met me, let alone the people that thought they 'knew' me but had really just seen me on the train to London once in a while. Many were the usual bitchy types, saying that I was just after a footballer's money – and they rolled out that old favourite 'WAG wannabe'. It just goes to show that some people will *always* pull you apart after you've been lumped into a certain category.

"I don't think I've ever really recovered from what was written about me and it still hurts if I ever hear people referring to that article." – Cassie Sumner

I wish I could say that was my only bad experience of the public's perception, but it wasn't. After I had my hideous time with *The Sun* and how they portrayed me, a load of gossip websites took the story and ran with it. The worst thing was that it was now out of my control. Although I managed, via the Press Complaints Commission, to get the story deleted from *The Sun*, I can do nothing about the following pieces and they still remain to this day.

When I look at them now, I can see that they're actually quite comical – but they still hurt when I first saw them, especially as they were entirely based on a story which wasn't true. I was about to write about where they came from, but I'd rather die than give these gutter sites any further publicity.

Read on, if you dare …

"The twenty-two-year-old PA/model is wearing a kaftan in the picture above, which is actually designed to be worn over a bikini on the beach. It now forms part of her arsenal of 'sluttish' dresses (her words, not mine), which are all bought from high street stores because ~~she's cheap~~ the footballers wouldn't notice the difference anyway."

"At the Christmas party she attended during a seven month stint with a Premier League love rat, Francesca saw girls removing their knickers in the toilets to 'up the ante', and said that many boasted of being 'gangbanged' the previous weekend. Sure Francesca. You *saw other* girls removing their knickers."

Now correct me if I'm wrong, but since when has it been a crime to mix up your clothes? Gok Wan does it all the time, and I'm pretty sure he'd fully advocate using a kaftan as a dress. I see girls do it all the time, it's really not that weird. And do I detect a little snobbery there about high street clothes? That's really not cool, you know, especially in the current economic climate. Not cool at all.

Not only that, but I've never, *ever* said I'm a model. There are thousands of amazing models – I'm not stupid enough to think it's a serious career path for too-short, too-ordinary, too-fat *moi*. I wouldn't be skinny enough, nor would I want to be. And finally – are you implying that it was *me* who was removing my underwear? Surely that's defamation or something? (I wish I'd paid more attention to law at college now.)

Although it *is* all rather comical, it just reinforces what I'm saying about how the media treats us girls – and, in turn, how the public will …

Aimee

A great example of how footballers' girls are unfairly portrayed is the Ashley Cole story – or, as *The Sun* put it, 'Colegate'. (It's literary genius, really.)

Aimee Walton, I salute you. She's endured hundreds of stories in the aftermath of her exclusive, calling her names you wouldn't even call a vicious criminal, when all she did was rather bravely try to give her side of the story about a man she alleges to be a liar and a cheat who wouldn't look out of place on *The Jeremy Kyle Show*.

Cheryl, on the other hand, was heralded as a saint. "How can something so bad happen to someone so beautiful?" the glossy weeklies incessantly enquired. They forget that, as demonstrated in several TV interviews, she does appear to have (as one witty journalist once put it) "the personality of a rattlesnake". Poor Cheryl, who apparently deserved so much better, is nothing more than a fame-hungry reality TV contestant (remember *Popstars: The Rivals?*), who interrupted her career with an allegedly racially-motivated attack on a toilet attendant which landed her in court. This was followed by several disgustingly scathing remarks to all manner of people (including Lily Allen) that can only be described as bullying. She berated Aimee in the national press for being a single mum and a hairdresser, when she should have been graciously thanking her (even if only in private) for exposing the state of her marriage.

The press didn't do poor Aimee any justice either. They focused on the fact that she apparently wasn't attractive enough, that you could see her roots, and that she supposedly wasn't up to scratch for precious Ashley. What on earth do they think they're proving by seeking to compare these two women in the beauty and wealth stakes?

As always, the footballer gets off looking like a bit of a rebellious stud, while the wife will pretend nothing's happened (see Coleen and the granny incident), or perhaps only acknowledge it by selling a couple of sombre-looking pictures to *OK*. It also bugs me how Cheryl berated Aimee for getting money from the scandal. Well *hello*, but do you really think she would have got that extremely lucrative *X-Factor* job without Colegate?

What really made me laugh is how so few people saw through what Cheryl and Ashley appeared to be doing. In my opinion she was never going to leave him! I don't believe all that stuff about going to Thailand to take a break and lose half her bodyweight, whilst pretending not to know the paps were waiting there for her. Then there was him going to Chinawhite in defiance of all the tabloids which slated him for being under the thumb. I was in there that night (it was a Wednesday – where else would I be?); he just sat at a secluded corner table looking bored with a few friends for an hour or two, then slunk off. His sole aim that night was to be pictured going in and out of there, as if to prove a point. *Well done, Ashley!*

What infuriates me, to the point where I just had to take some Rescue Remedy, is how Aimee came out of all this. I've nothing but respect and admiration for that girl. No, she's not perfect, and yes, she did wrong – but she's certainly shown more morality and self-restraint than Cheryl, and probably you and I put together.

Yes, I'm including myself in this, and do you know why? Although I didn't ever name Wesley in the press, I totally milked that story for all it was worth. I used him and the situation to my advantage, to gain what I wanted. In my case it was a book deal – something I'd always wanted. I never imagined that this is what my debut book would be about, and in a way I hate even hearing the words 'WAG' or 'footballer' – but its also something that's become a personal mission for me now.

Aimee said one thing that really stood out to me, something that any girl who's had dealings of this kind could relate to. And that was that she could have simply accepted a pay-off far higher than what the paper had offered her, but she turned it down. Why? Because as a mother and as a woman, she wanted to show Cheryl what her husband was really like.

She also wanted to show Ashley that you don't mess with a blonde and get away with it, and the only way she could realistically do that was via the national press. Everyone ridiculed her, saying that she was in it for the fame and the money, ignoring any sense of personal morality or her anger at how she'd been treated. Well, actions speak louder, and what Aimee did next impresses me beyond comprehension. She did nothing. Not one interview, not one feature. Nothing.

Now, I know that with a tiny bit of public interest you can spin that one story, which might not be particularly solid anyway (look at me – we didn't even name him!), into lots of other opportunities. After *The Sun* totally slated me I had telegrams delivered to my house for weeks afterwards, asking for interviews for women's weeklies and glossy monthlies. I did everything from *Woman* to *Grazia*, TV, radio – I did it all! If you strike while the iron is hot then it can be lucrative, and even get you the right kind of press. Lots of girls simply want to be a glamour model (because we don't have enough of those, right?) and this is their way of standing out among thousands of other blonde identikits

My point is that Cheryl appears to have benefited enormously out of this, as it's raised her profile much higher than that of her bandmates. Amy has still never said another word, to the best of my knowledge. She's a young single mother and works in what I imagine is a hard job with relatively low pay. I'm not sure I could have sat back and taken everything that was thrown at me in that situation. Hell, I don't think I could even in the situation I'm in now! So Aimee, if you're reading this – not everyone hates you. In fact I commend you, and urge others to take a look at your side of the story too.

Come to think of it, Cheryl has a little WAG don't-wannabe charm about her too. Okay, so her husband allegedly cheated with several women and the whole world knows about it. But now, a few months on, she's got one of the best jobs in British light-entertainment TV and her profile is higher than ever. She turned that negative into a big, fat positive.

She didn't actually have the balls to dump the guy, but she could still shed about twenty million tears on *The X-Factor* as contestant after contestant told of how their mothers/fathers/wives/husbands/cats had died. Of course, this was all rounded off with neat editing and sad background music to really set the scene. As Cheryl herself admits, this has been the best year ever for her, career-wise. Funny that, isn't it?

Another great example is Rebecca Loos. Even after all this time, the papers can't help but have cruel digs at her. *The Mirror*, just a few days ago, described Miss Loos as 'Queen of Chavs'. I'm sorry, but how so? Since when did being a multilingual graduate with a diplomat for a father make you a chav? Words fail me, and at times like this I don't see any point in trying to change people's minds about us girls, and making them see it's the footballers who are the skanky hos – not us.

Ding Dong, the Witch Is Dead!
Dealing with Bad Press

It's Sunday morning; you've woken up with the birds to be among the first to see your story in its full double-page, multi-coloured glory before anyone else! On first glance, it's quite usual to be annoyed with the headline, some quotes or even your picture, but you must realise that you're going to be much more critical than anyone else who's reading. You are your own worst judge – so try not to fret! Having said that, tabloids will be tabloids and they don't have that reputation for nothing. So be prepared for at least a little bad press.

Almost every single time I've done a piece of press, I always seem to shout out, "*NOOOOOOO!*" very loudly upon first setting eyes on it. Even when I was having a rather intelligent and well-articulated debate (so I thought, anyway) with Ian Wright's ex-wife, in a women's magazine, they lifted one tiny quote and splashed it all across the page in bright pink letters, sending the rest of the article into obscurity. The quote? "Footballers are just a notch on the bedpost." I didn't actually say that.

Well, I did – but in the context of: "It appears that footballers are just a notch on the bedpost for a lot of girls." But of course, as always, they made it sound like it was all about me. Can it get any worse? Well yes, actually. Take *The Sun*. They hadn't told me exactly when they were publishing the story and, as I happily sat on the tube, oblivious, everyone else was reading a screaming *Sun* headline that declared me to be depraved.

Although I always say my experience with *The People* was *almost* pleasant, and that I felt they looked after me well, there was still a part that absolutely makes me cringe to this day! With all tabloid tales, however nice the journalists and editors are, it's dirt and sordidness that the readers really want. I have never thought about it until now, but it's odd how men and women up and down the country may have read all about my sex life with Wesley. That doesn't bother me so much, as I don't even know these people. But it's strange to think of people I went to school with, or friends, family and colleagues, reading it. I still can't believe that a kiss-and-tell story in which I *didn't* tell made front-page news. And of course the headline was simply, 'GAGGED!' Upon first seeing it, you could be forgiven for thinking it was a piece about kinky bondage games.

I've told you the whole story of what happened with Wesley now, so I'll show you how the kiss-and-tell came out. Although there are things that I'm unhappy with or are not quite right, I don't feel it's actually that bad at all. (If *you* think it's bad then you should see how some kiss-and-tells are reported.)

"A cheating premiership star posed as a stripper called Wesley to bed a secretary [*I'm a PA actually, thank you very much*] behind his girlfriend's back.

"The international player [*in more than ways than one*]

was so scared of being caught playing away [*see what they did there?*] with sexy [*why, thank you!*] Francesca Amber Sawyer that he ..."

As with all tabloids, they must use a series of bullet points with the first word emboldened in capitals to really state their point. I remember seeing Russell Brand talk about these in one of his stand-up routines, and it really is hilarious which words they choose to emphasise. Mine were:

"PRETENDED he was a stripper before reluctantly admitting after sex he was a fan's favourite.

"USED his girlfriend's car so he wouldn't be spotted arriving for weekly romps in his easily-recognised supercar ...

"ORDERED Francesca to check his naked body and clothes for her tell-tale blonde hairs before he left ...

"Francesca, 22 who had a seven-month fling with the star told *The People*: 'When I met him he told me he was single and a stripper called Wesley. It was only after we slept together that he confessed he was a soccer player earning tens of thousands every week [*he never quoted his salary, for Christ's sake!*] with a partner and child.' ...

"Francesca met the player earlier this year in trendy ***** nightclub in Kensington ...

"After a month of phone contact the pair met at a pal's flat in London's Royal Docks and their first date turned into a five-hour sex session. [*Oh my God, my dad's read this!*]

"Francesca recalled: [*someone shut me up, please!*] 'I was asking him questions about his personal life [*right to the point, as ever!*] and I noticed that he'd often pause for ages as if he was thinking up a lie. He told me he would end up marrying his girlfriend one day but he felt trapped.

"'I made the first move [*I bloody didn't!*] because it had got to 4am and he was so shy I thought he'd never get around to it.

"'We were on his mate's bed when I started kissing him and he was immediately aroused [*thanks for that!*] … He was near-perfect in bed [*that's true – my friend Holly asked me, if I could sleep with Wesley again or Kanye West, who would it be? This is cruel, as I LOVE Kanye West. But I chose Wesley. Cringe.*]

"'We were having sex until 9am in all sorts of different positions and he was throwing me around the bed [*is this getting a little too graphic for anyone, or is it just me?*] …

"After sleeping with Francesca for the first time the player came clean about his herpes … [*I'm totally kidding!*] … his true identity …

"'I asked him why he'd lied and he said he wanted a girl who liked him for him and not because he is a footballer.' [*Fair enough.*]

NERVOUS [*what kind of bloody subtitle is that?*]

"Francesca chose not to show the player the red card [*woohoo, see what they did there? Classic tabloid stuff!*]. A week later she met him again – this time at her friend's flat in the City of London …

"'… [He] was obsessed about being seen or getting a parking ticket. He said he'd never be able to explain to his partner why he was in the City … [*Checking out the stock market, buying some shares, doing some banking? Damn, you're right, you could never explain being in an area not filled with clubs, bars and strip joints. My bad.*]

"'He doesn't like to start sex [*that's so not true!*] so I led him into the bedroom. It's like he feels if the girl takes the lead then it's not all his fault so he doesn't feel guilty [*go figure that logic, girls!*].' ...

"Francesca decided to end it with the star earlier this month after realising she was getting emotionally involved [*sob, sob*].

"She said: 'It's frustrating that he goes home to his partner. He promised to see me more but they were just empty promises [*no shit, Sherlock!*].'"

As you can see, even if they're little minor things, when they're personal to you they seem to stick out like Peter Crouch at a dwarf revue. No one else will even notice though – so stop freaking out.

> *"I was reading so much about myself in the papers that was just not true."* – Rebecca Loos

It's not the tabloids themselves who are your worst enemies. I was branded a 'WAG wannabe' – a term I detest and reject in equal measures – by those gossip websites, and it's attracted the nastiest of comments ever since. That's the thing with these sites, they're registered by proper weirdoes who just sit there and make nasty comment on every story that comes up. I like to think they're slightly tubby men in their mid-forties who still live with their mums, and hate women because they've never known the love of one. The good news (if you're a glass half-full kinda girl) is that they write this kind of stuff about *everyone*, so I don't take it to heart anymore.

I once posted a link to the Press Complaints Commission website, detailing how the story in *The Sun* had been removed and how it had never been my intention to be involved with footballers in the way that I'm now perceived to have been, but still they trashed me for weeks after.

I find the best way to deal with bad press is, first of all, to look at it objectively. Are you just being oversensitive? Ask your friends and family for an honest opinion. Hopefully, more and more people these days are becoming more media-savvy than ever before, and know that lots of stuff in the papers is either elaborated upon or just totally made up.

Approach the Press Complaints Commission if you really think you have a viable claim. Although the damage has been done now and everyone has read it over their Sunday fry-up, you can still get an apology or have the story pulled from the paper's website. Although I managed to have my most damaging story removed, it pains me to think that, no matter what I say now, Wesley has read it and will think that's what I said and that's what I am. No amount of retractions can put a price on the trust that was lost then.

You can also follow up with more sympathetic coverage if you really feel you've been portrayed badly. I did this by appearing in a few other magazines and as a guest, along with Charley Uchea and Nicola T, on *Richard and Judy*.

WAG Don't-Wannabe

Richard and Judy were lovely, and really allowed me to get my point across. (As much as you can with Charley Uchea sharing the couch with you!) At the time when I did that show I was at my lowest point. Wesley and I had finished, I was being slated in the press, and no one could understand my fury at the whole situation. To top it all off, it was my 23rd birthday.

That day turned it around for me. As I sat speaking to a fellow guest in the green room, former *Sun* editor Kelvin McKenzie, about the idea for my book, I got my first positive response. He really could see me as the girl-done-wrong who simply made the mistake of falling for the wrong boy, instead of the blonde gold-digger the tabloids loved to paint me as.

Unfortunately the press just love to hate some people. Look at poor old Jordan, they used to slate her for years – it's only in recent times that they've come around to loving 'Katie Price'. Another is Rebecca Loos, who for some strange reason is very close to my heart. She is still tarred with the 'homewrecking chav' tag all these years later, despite being a grounded, beautiful and educated woman. That's what an affair with a footballer can do to you.

And Beckham? Well, he's still our golden boy, isn't he?

RESEARCH, REVELATIONS AND REASONS TO BOYCOTT FOOTBALLERS FOR GOOD

April 2008

Last night a friend of mine, Holly, and I went to Aura with an American pro-basketballer friend of hers. That place is ghetto, it's crazy! Anyway, just as we were about to leave, I saw the tallest man I've ever seen (*God, I just love tall men!*) point to me, and before I knew it some burly minder-type with Austin Powers glasses had pulled me back and ushered me into a private booth with him. Luckily for me he was a bit of a hottie, and I found out he was a massively famous pro football player in the USA.

Normally I would be a little ghetto myself, just give him a 'whatever' and walk away. I mean, a man who grabs my attention by grabbing *me* really isn't my bag, baby! But, purely for research purposes, I decided to go along with it and experience what it's like to know a man is a famous baller from the very start, seeing a guy purely through his on-pitch credentials. After all, I've been writing about it for so long now, and have given so many opinions of the girls that do it, but I'd never really been in that situation myself. It was fun!

The two minders, my friend, he and I went back to an after-party at the hotel in Kensington where his whole team were staying. Yes, that's right – I did a hotel room after-party in true hussy style! Anyway, I shan't divulge what went on that night, but I swear it's nowhere near as bad as what you're thinking (probably).

The footballer, who we shall name Marc, had to leave for the airport at 6:00am the next morning but Holly and I slept in. As we woke up and abused the room service, we watched *Jeremy Kyle* and laughed at the guests. The situations they found themselves in were ridiculous and I couldn't help but sneer when one woman exclaimed, "I know my daughter's safe on the street – she's with my drug dealer!" or another proclaimed, "I don't know which brother is my baby's father."

We laughed at the pregnant teenage guests with messy love lives that invariably involved other family members, but as I watched I realised that it's just life in varying degrees. *Jeremy Kyle* IS life for all of us – there are just varying degrees of separation. Even though I consider myself and those around me far removed from it, in reality the same stories are played out everywhere across the country.

Just because the guys we slept with were famous, and the boyfriends we cheated on were rich, it didn't make the situation any better. While they got it on in an alleyway, we had sex games in five-star hotels; while they drove Ford Escorts and picked up the dole, our men drove Bentleys and Maybachs and picked up table bills that ran into thousands. Just because the guy I had an affair with was a footballer and my boyfriend a wealthy club owner, and we maintained our illicit affair in a prime-located Square Mile apartment, it didn't *really* make it any more classy than those who were carrying on with their cross-eyed brother-in-law from the council house next door.

Only money made what these footballers got up to night after night seem credible, and girls were risking their careers by having their involvement in it splashed across the news. I realised then how important it was for me, in order to write this book in a balanced way, to really get inside what I'm talking about. I decided there and then to go to every party, to get naked at every opportunity and to massage every ego. I wanted insider information – and boy, did I get it.

> *"Naked research? Who was the lucky footballer this time? This must be the best researched book ever!"*
> – Gareth Morgan, tabloid journalist

The second guy I met on my journey was David. (No, it's not Beckham. No such luck.). After a night of naked note-taking our relationship came to an abrupt halt, as coaches and managers demanded full concentration from their players. I made my way back to London via a short walk of shame through the hotel lobby and a one-hour car ride.

As always with these footballers, it turned out that naughty David had a girlfriend and a child.[*] I initially found out by way of trusty old Facebook. We had a couple of mutual friends and one of them had posted pictures of the 'happy couple'. When I questioned somebody about it later, he replied nonchalantly that yes, David had a girlfriend and a one-year-old baby. He said it like it was the most normal thing in the world for a relatively new dad to do. It still strikes me dumb and makes me despair every time. I chose never to speak to David again.

I didn't mind so much that he was so careless – he was like that by nature, and also very open, so I knew it was never going to go any further. Nor did I ever want it to. The situation couldn't have been more different from that of Wesley. With Wesley I felt terribly betrayed and let down – with David it was just research material.

Could my heart have turned as cold and stony as those of the guys I'm studying? Maybe.

Fun-Time Frankie – A European Misadventure

> *"Nobody in the game of football should be called a genius. A genius is someone like Norman Einstein."*
> – Joe Theismann, American football player

Soon after meeting David I got a mysterious phone call. The call was from a world-famous young player who I shall call

---

[*] *As usual, it just seemed to slip his mind until it was too late.*

Frankie. How did he get my number? David gave it to him of course (number/girl swapping is rife amongst footballers), and he assumed he could just call me and get instant booty time. *I don't think so.*

Frankie and I had met back in the summer, when I got invited to the American national football team's party at one of my favourite London nightspots, Paper. In case you think of me as terribly calculating, I'm afraid I wasn't that clever (or even bothered), as I was actually partying the night away in Chinawhite at the time. A promoter I know who is always wherever the footballers are came in and begged my friends and I to come to a party around the corner, promising us it would be super fun.

Some fun. We turned up and it was basically a roomful of blinged-up ballers and a very drunk Danielle Lloyd. But there was an after-party at a hotel where the whole team were staying. Ah, now it's all coming back …

When one of the footballers and I walked into a room it was like a scene from a particularly debauched Snoop Dogg video. Two naked girls were lying on the bed and something that looked suspiciously like a crack pipe was being smoked in the bathroom. We stayed and chatted for about five minutes but were quite keen to get out. Still, all sorts of names, rumours and classic quotes aplenty were being thrown about, and the journalistic side of me just couldn't help myself. Before I knew it I was reaching over (discreetly, I drunkenly thought) to grab a pen and one of those pads with the hotel's name and address on it, and began frantically scribbling whatever I could remember. This book isn't about naming and shaming, so I needn't have bothered – but I felt incredibly Martin Bashir-esque at the time.

One of the girls demanded rather rudely to know what I was writing. I think she was antsy because she was fat and naked, and I was fully clothed. I styled it out by claiming, "I'm on crack! Ha ha! I'm just writing rubbish!" This blonde crack addict act has won many a fool over, and I showed her my notes just to prove it. (I was writing in shorthand, which to the untrained eye looks like a load of scribbles.) Lucky escape. She didn't look like the sort of girl you wanted to meet down a dark alley. Or indeed naked in bed, as I had the misfortune to.

One of the guys I met that night was Frankie. Frankie is seriously HUGE in America, as I found out courtesy of Google. We spoke briefly, and when I say briefly I mean literally a drunken 'hiya' across the room before we moved on. A couple of days later I had a call from a number I didn't recognise. It was Frankie.

As with most Americans, and most teenagers (he was both, I'm ashamed to say), he wanted to talk for hours on the phone. He said how much he missed me, and I pondered how this was possible as we barely knew each other. What was there to miss?

Despite his youth I found him endearing and, research aside, grew to love talking to him. After a month or two of long transatlantic phone calls, he eventually persuaded me to go out and visit him where his new football club were situated, in a beautiful part of Europe. Initially I wasn't willing to go at all, never mind alone but the more we talked the more I got to like him. I finally agreed, with him booking the flights for a friend and I to fly out that very Friday.

(It was a bank holiday weekend, which swayed me. Why waste a perfectly good Monday when you could be sunbathing and sipping cocktails by the pool just to stay in London for it to rain, as it *always* does on a bank holiday?)

As I Googled Frankie and the ******* football team, and packed my bikini, I started to realise that, although I liked him, I couldn't let myself get hurt again. That's why I took Holly, and decided to look on the weekend as a little field trip to gain a more rounded insight of the world I'm writing about.

I felt a pang of guilt at my calculated motives. He had asked me out to spend time with him, and to see him play, and I was treating him as nothing more than a lab rat. Just then I received a text from Frankie, saying, "I can't wait for you to get here so I can f*** you in the a** the minute you arrive – can I do that? Also I don't want to wear a c***** – I hate them." (By the way, the answer to both was a firm, "NO!")

Suddenly I didn't feel so bad. I remembered why I feel like I do about these guys. So let the games begin!

After the minor mishap of missing our flight and therefore missing Frankie before he was packed off to the team hotel before the game, Holly and I arrived. Sun, sea, beautiful scenery and our skin begging to be tanned – we were ready for a good time!

We settled into Frankie's room and ordered ourselves room service – a romantic dinner for two blondes on the balcony. Not quite how I had pictured my supposed 'dirty weekend' with Frankie. The days passed in a blur of sunbathing, eating, watching football in a stadium full of crazy French fans, drinking copious amounts of vodka, going to a club in Cannes, accidentally flashing about 200 people and inadvertently bringing a Spanish prostitute back to our table – rather like my old cat, who used to bring in all manner of undesirable objects for us to get rid of.

Frankie himself was adorable at times, but definitely had some undesirable footballer characteristics. I'd written about footballers so much over the last few months, yet hadn't spent more than twenty-four hours in their company at any one time – how was I going to handle four days straight with him? The answer was, I didn't.

He drove me insane. It was like living with a moody teenager, which I guess is exactly what he was. He swung from, "Let's get naked, I want you so much my little snowflake [I'm not joking – I wish I was!], I'm falling for you, come live with me," to "Oh my goodness, you British bitches are driving me crazy! You just wild out like, all the time! I can't speak to you. Your accents are driving me nuts!"

(We were doing Amy Winehouse impressions at the time, which I don't think Americans can quite get: "I'd rather have cat-Aids, thank you very much, I said, '*No, no, noooooo-ah!*'") At one point we seriously ignored each other for about twenty-four hours straight. That's really hard when you're in the same room and sharing everything, including bed space.

Ah, bed space. That's how we came to not speaking in the first place.

On the night we went to Cannes, I can safely say that I got more drunk than I ever have been in my entire life. That says a lot, because, as you can probably see from the remainder of this book, I drink a lot. I was drinking glasses that were 80 percent Grey Goose vodka and just fifteen percent Red Bull. (The other five percent is unidentified to this day.) I downed three so fast that, not only had they barely touched the sides, but everyone else had barely touched their first.

Anyway, as you can probably predict, the night ended incredibly messily, with me declaring that the little old Romanian woman selling roses outside the club was really my mum and almost being sick on the way back. All I remember next is waking up with the most incredible pain in my stomach, the worst headache in the universe and the feeling that I was made 100 percent from dust. (Actually, scrap that – 90 percent dust and ten percent asbestos.) It was gross.

As I staggered around the room trying to find a drink, any drink, I noticed I was also completely butt-naked. I also had that feeling that I'd definitely not been sleeping the night before. I don't know how I was capable of anything at all, but apparently I was. As I lay there, wishing for the world to end so that this pain would stop, Fun-Time Frankie decided it was time for round two. Or, perhaps more realistically, round eleven. (Goddamn energetic teenagers!) *Ding ding!*

I really was in no mood for any of this nonsense, but

footballers will be footballers and he was used to getting his own way 100 percent of the time. The upshot of our rather tedious and nauseating half-hour of petty arguing was twenty-four hours of 'grumpy Frankie', who refused to talk to Holly and I.

It's all the 'yes' people who have surrounded him for all of his short adult life, pandering to his every whim, that had given him this notion of self-importance. He really couldn't believe that there would be a girl out there who *didn't* want to just pleasure him for every waking (or sleeping) hour.

I Can't Speak French

> *"It is a truth universally acknowledged, that a single man in possession of a good fortune, must be in want of a wife."* – Jane Austen, *Pride and Prejudice*

My favourite was a French Premiership footballer who I shall call Pierre, as that's a French name and I have no imagination. He had been on a night out with a bunch of his team-mates, one of whom Holly was seeing casually. On the particular night he was there, I'd been back home in Essex to babysit my little dog, Charlie-Lou. (Damn you, Charlie! You really could have looked after yourself, you had those one-portion, easy-tear packets of dogmeat.)

So I didn't go that night, but the various footballers, including Pierre, began to add my friends to their friends on Facebook. As I am in a lot of their pictures (it's not often I miss a night out) he must have thought I was there too, and sent me the following message: "When am I going to see you again?"

Again? I thought. This boy really is a prime project if ever I saw one!

By now I was really into the world of footballers. Weekends away, invites to matches, nights out, etc. I wanted to keep the ball rolling (this tabloid style is really catching!), partially because I wanted to get the most rounded perspective that I possibly could, to be fair to them. But it was also because I was enjoying myself so much – more than I ever had with my primary reason for writing this book, Wesley.

That's the thing about footballers. With them you can do anything you want and go anywhere you want without having to surround yourself with red-cheeked, Stowe-educated, Mustique-going Hooray Henrys. The type who crowd Boujis and Whiskey Mist, with their coma-inducing banter and sickening snobbery, looking down on the footballers with bewilderment and disdain, wondering what on earth these untitled, new-money, state-school, working-class men could have that impresses the ladies more than they do.

But that's exactly it. It's NEW money. No snobbery. No affectedness. Just fun!

Anyway, back to Pierre. This guy looked hot, so I played along. He was asking for my number when we'd only been speaking for about five minutes. I refused to give it to him, but every time I logged on there he was, asking me for my digits again. One night, a few weeks after we'd first spoken, I decided he was pretty sweet and finally relented. Straight away I got a phone call.

This happened on and off most nights and we always found plenty to say, although he spoke broken English and I spoke smashed-to-smithereens French. He was due in London for a couple of days and asked me out on a date one Thursday night.

An actual date, a dinner date – not a 'let's get naked' date. I couldn't believe it. A footballer? A civilised dinner? These are the sorts of activities I usually reserve for property developers and the like. Maybe I had judged these guys too soon. As a party-loving blonde with silicone enhancement I get my fair share of stereotyping, and I have to admit that I hate it. Was I guilty of the same offence with footballers?

It gave me new hope that maybe they weren't *all* bad, and that I was about to see a very different side to the world of football.

Thursday night rolled around, and I settled upon a safe, simple yet sexy outfit of skinny black jeans, high leopard-print heels, a little black corset and a tiny shrug. I wore my hair loose and long, with the help of the odd extension or two, was pretty tanned from my trip to Europe, and sprayed myself liberally with my favourite perfume. I was ready!

Unfortunately, Pierre was not. He was an hour late. A full HOUR! Normally I would have refused to go after this feckless timekeeping, but maybe Pierre had some important footballer duties to attend to: such as a spot of dogging on the way, taking a DNA test for an angry single mother, preparing a 'roast' or watching slow-motion action replays of himself on repeat.

He eventually came to pick me up and off we went to Trader Vic's, in the basement of the Hilton Hotel on Park Lane (my choice). The cocktails in there are to die for and the place is super-cute, relatively casual for a cosy date. We turned up to about fifteen circling and snapping paparazzi. Pierre wasn't happy and seemed rather eager to just get into the restaurant.

Dinner was gorgeous, and I made up for his abstinence from alcohol by having vodka in everything that I ordered, including the organic apple juice. He surprised me with how sweet and shy he was, and I started to warm to him more than I'd ever expected. He then dropped the bombshell: he was a Muslim and didn't believe in sex before marriage.

Surely not? I began to question him on the Eleven Pillars of Islam, but he seemed keen to move on, insisting he wasn't a Koran-bashing fanatic. Okay, but he was claiming to be celibate and I was suspicious.

Moving on as swiftly as Sienna Miller from Rhys Ifans to Balthazar Getty, he described a 'hilarious' time when his agent brought two girls out to dinner with him to meet Pierre, almost like he was their pimp. They wanted to have a threesome with him (which is obviously something you discuss at the dinner table upon first meeting!), but he didn't want to because he was tired. Instead, being the gentleman that he is, he discreetly asked them to follow him to the toilets – that's right, readers, the *toilets* of the restaurant – where he wanted them both to give him, ahem, joint oral pleasure. Except he didn't put it quite so nicely.

Aha! So here we are! The true footballer emerges from beneath his Muslim/celibate façade. Amazingly, when I questioned his conflicting actions he simply said that oral sex doesn't count. Okay …

He also told me all about his son and the mother of the child, who lives back in his hometown with his parents. He's only seen his son twice since he was born, and told me how the mother often cries when she sees him and begs him to take her back. He just laughs and says no.

There but for the grace of God go I …

When it came to leaving he didn't want to walk out the front door of the hotel, so the restaurant manager who had followed us up arranged for a taxi to meet us at the back. Just then the paparazzi burst through the doors and began to take pictures of us at the reception desk. Now it looked like we were booking into a room. Poor old Pierre! They were ordered out but met us once again outside the back door, where things got so crazy that Pierre hit his head on a lens, I tripped over a pap who was lying on the floor (don't ask!) and one guy jumped in our taxi door, snapping all the way for about 100 meters down the road.

We laughed the whole way to Nobu, where he refused to get out because of all the photographers waiting outside. I couldn't see the problem myself, they'd already pictured him in a hotel with a blonde – surely that was the worst that could happen? I later found out that it wasn't that he had a secret girlfriend or anything like that, but rather that his manager is notoriously strict, and if he saw him out late on a weeknight, a few days before a game, he'd go mad – especially as it was only his first week at the new club. Despite him not drinking all night, even ordering a Pina Colada with no alcohol, it didn't look good for him.

At the time of writing this I've seen Pierre a few times and, although I really do hate to admit it, he's slowly growing on me. Am I really falling for him though, or am I just doing it to wind up Wesley? They know each other fairly well and, from past experience, I know that my seeing anyone else drives Wesley crazy. Nevertheless, Pierre is quite a cutie in his own right.

I know, I know! I know what you're going to say, that I promised myself after the nightmare that was Wesley that I would never, ever, be foolish enough to fall for a footballer again, and you're right. But with Wesley, I was just blinded by my feelings for him and was quite naïve about the world of the Premiership footballer. I think I've definitely earned my stripes now, and can make a more educated decision.

Speaking of education, I've just realised that I've not even told you half of the things I've seen and heard on my travels ...

Facebook Detective

*"The internet is like alcohol in some sense.
It accentuates what you would do anyway."*
– Esther Dyson, quoted in *Time* magazine

Just recently my friends and I have been going out quite a bit with a couple of players from a big London club. They're always tons of fun, we've been going out to dinner or to clubs, getting wasted, and naturally assumed that they were all single. After all, isn't this how singletons act?

A friend of mine, who I shall call Grace, had been very casually seeing one of the players both out in public and in a more intimate sense over the last couple of weeks. He was kind of hot, even if he did have funny hair, and, despite our rules about getting too close to footballers, she admitted that she quite liked him. After seeing each other a couple of times, they decided to throw caution to the wind and stop using protection – which, as a girl, is not a step I would have taken lightly. In fact, I would only do it if the definite subtext was, "We're going to be doing this a lot, only with each other, and I trust you."

Imagine her shock when, just the other day, she got a message on Facebook from a girl claiming to be his long-term girlfriend! Somehow, through various people (remember it's a small world, and everyone seems to know everyone else's business), she found out about their little liaisons, located Grace online and contacted her, wanting to know the truth.

WAG Don't-Wannabe

My friend refused to reply, which I think was definitely the right thing to do. The girlfriend in question is, totally by chance, some skank I went to a party in Africa with once. She was proper weird, saying she was Brazilian when her accent was pure cockney, and wore *white hot pants* with stilettos to the airport.

(To the airport! Even Victoria Beckham admits that she flies in her pyjamas. Besides, who the hell are you going to see in a tiny airport in the middle of Africa?)

So anyway, as it stands, my friend is refusing to break her trust and reveal anything to the girlfriend. The girlfriend probably won't dump him anyway. She'll say something about not having any "concrete evidence", and that Grace is simply "a skanky ho boyfriend-stealer". But to my mind, the minute you have to email a random girl to ask her what your boyfriend's been up to is a very sad day indeed. I think that kind of answers any question you have anyway. She's definitely *not* a WAG don't-wannabe. Grace, on the other hand, has learnt her lesson and cut off all contact with the rat.

I wish that was a one-off case, but it isn't. My other friend, who I shall call Allegra, met a hot guy in a club one night. They began to see each other so often that even I ended up staying at his house a few times a week. Whenever we would go out he'd always come and pick us up, wherever we were. He was tall, sweet and played for the same team as Wesley. (See what I mean about it being a small world?) We would all often camp over there for *après*-club sleepovers, watching TV and eating all his food. It was fun, and he seemed genuine. Allegra was smitten.

One of these nights she found a bracelet on the bedside table, and asked, jokingly, "Whose is this? Your girlfriend's?" To which he replied, "Yes, it is." He'd been with her for about a year. He felt absolutely no guilt in what he was doing to either her or Allegra, not even enough to try to cover it up.

I often find that a lot of footballers feel there's absolutely nothing wrong with what they're doing. There are so many girls giving them exactly what they want, without question, that they feel it's their God-given right. What they've forgotten is that these are real lives they're playing with, especially where naïve younger girls are concerned, what with all the unprotected sex and babies flying about. [*]

Which brings us swiftly back to Pierre. He delightfully informed me at dinner last week that he has a baby, to which I exclaimed incredulously, "Really?!" "Of course I do, everyone has a baby," he replied without even a hint of irony.

I would tell you the name of this poor, godforsaken child if I could, because you would laugh until you cry. But I can't, and won't. Not only do many of these footballing fathers seem not to give two hoots about the children they thoughtlessly bring into this world and the women that bear them, they also seem intent on giving them ludicrous names that even Bob Geldof would declare barmy.

That's the thing that still shocks me so much about these guys. I'm definitely not lumping them all into one category,

* Not literally, of course. That would be crazy.

but for the vast majority, even a woman having their child isn't enough to earn their attention and respect. For me, as a woman, I feel that's just about the biggest thing I can give of myself to anyone. Bigger than marriage, monogamy – hell, even giving away a kidney! Once you have a child, that's it – your body and mind are never the same again, and for the rest of your life you're 'a woman with a child from a previous relationship'. I never want to be that.

The fact that the amazing miracle of life isn't enough to make a footballer stop, think and take his dick out of the girl he just met in a club, or on Facebook, astounds me, and is the biggest reason why I will never, ever marry one.

The amount of things I've experienced, that have happened to friends of mine or even to me, would take me ten years to write about. Unfortunately, the deadline for this book is now upon me.

But from what I've already told you, hopefully you are on your way to making a more educated choice about dating a footballer. Maybe you think the money and the lifestyle will be more fun than you can imagine, or maybe, at the other end of the scale, you're wondering if one of the guys I'm writing about is *your* boyfriend or husband. All I can tell you is what I've witnessed – and it doesn't look good.

I am pleased, however, that it's backed up everything that I thought I knew all along.

EXTRA TIME ...
THE AFTERMATH

"With a player like you, I don't have a prayer ..."–
'Too Little Too Late' by Jojo, allegedly written about
ex-boyfriend, international footballer Freddy Adu.

They think it's all over. It is now. You've done the deed, cut
him out of your life, but you feel like you can't go on ...

That feeling you have after a significant relationship has
come to an end never gets easier, even with age. As I've gotten
older I've realised that it *will* pass, and you won't always feel
like you want to just die in a pool of your own vomit – but
when the feeling bears down on you, it's still just as strong.

Unfortunately, getting your friends round for a bottle of
wine, with a stack of tissues at hand, whilst they tell you
earnestly, "He's an ugly shit anyway, no one will want him,
he is going to regret this *so much*," just isn't going to cut it.
He'll have a queue of up-for-it ladies right round the block.

It's not quite your average break-up; a night out, a drunken kiss with a randomer and a day of watching *Bridget Jones* in your pyjamas isn't going to work this time.

So how do you get over that special one? Well, it's not easy, and it's made all the harder when they're famous and reminders of them are everywhere you look.

When you break up with a regular guy, it's very easy to just cut him out of your life and quickly forget all about him. Out of sight is out of mind. It's just like that part in the film *The Beach*, when a guy gets attacked by a shark that leaves him with half a leg hanging off. The rest of the group can't handle his screams 24/7 and refuse to disclose their secret location by getting a doctor to see him. So they ship him off to the outskirts of the island and leave him to die there, where no one can hear him. That very same night they're drinking and laughing like before.

That's all very well with a regular guy – you might bump into him one night in a club and have a little relapse, a day or so of crying, Google-stalking his new girlfriend and listening to the whole of James Blunt's suicide-inducing album on repeat. But then you're done. You can pretty much avoid him forever. With a famous ex it's repeatedly shoved in your face at the most unexpected moments.

I'm not ashamed now to admit it's taken me a long time to get over Wesley. I was still only just 22 when I met him – old enough to know better, you may be thinking, but emotionally I was still incredibly young. I'd never had any real feelings for a guy before, even long-term boyfriends, and had sometimes been called 'the ice maiden', but this one hit me hard. Its being a secret affair probably didn't help – we all know the rule of wanting something you can't have.

Part of the reason it's taken me so long to get over him is there was never any final resolution. I always thought Americans were talking shit when they went on about 'needing closure', but it really is true. My tabloid story was supposed to serve the purpose of cutting our relationship dead in its tracks, never to be resurrected. It didn't quite work that way though, did it?

He still carried on seeing me for some time afterwards, and, after the second attempt to completely rid him from my life forever, he only stopped speaking to me for a few months. Getting back in contact with me all those months later, suggesting we start up our relationship again, was enough to send me crazy and definitely hindered my progress in moving on.

Wesley was always quite a quiet man and was never interested in courting publicity. However, since we finished our relationship he's been in the papers for being drunken disorderly, getting naked and just being generally crazy. This always seems to happen on the very same nights at the very same places where I'm due to attend, but for some reason have cancelled. My sister swears it's fate, that God is saying we are destined not to meet again, and maybe she's right.

Now, if ever I cancel a night out, sure enough, there he is in the papers the next day. I feel so weird about it now, and have had so many near misses, that I feel that if we ever did meet again, something crazy would happen – maybe one of us would spontaneously combust.

Just the other day I was minding my own business, making my way home to my little house in Camden from my office whilst reading the paper. As I turned over to the party pages, who should I see but Wesley coming out of my favourite club, stained, drunk and messy. I gasped audibly and several people around me flinched, as if I was about to self-detonate. I wanted to tell someone, to show them his picture and for them to tell me what a useless lout he was, and how I'm lucky to have seen the back of him. Unfortunately, London can be a pretty lonely place and the unwritten law is that strangers on the tube just don't chat.

Powerless to stop it, I suddenly had hundreds of emotions rushing back at me and felt like I'd been transported back in time. I thought about him for a day or two, but then soon forgot. It's definitely getting easier as time goes on, but things like this just keep on bringing it back to you.

Last night I was getting ready to go out with some friends, so we had some drinks to begin with. The boys were watching a big game on TV and Wesley happened to be playing. Afterwards, they conducted a couple of interviews and one was with Wesley … SHIRTLESS!

Why, oh why … ?

Headline Hunters

If you've cut off your relationship via a nice, juicy, revenge-seeking leak to the press, then you may be feeling the force of some pretty strong disapproval right now. Ride it out. People forgive and forget, and you've not killed anyone. If things are going well, capitalise on it and do some further press. As Max Clifford said about Rebecca Loos, yes, people she will never meet hated her for a bit, but she made a real nest egg for herself, an opportunity to purchase a home and to do something with her life she would otherwise never have had the chance to.

Even if you've received negative press you can always get something out of it. Sometimes it's good for people to hate you – just look at Victoria Beckham – as long as they'll still pay to listen to what you have to say.

Show Me the Money!

> *"A large income is the best recipe for happiness I ever heard of."* – Jane Austen, *Mansfield Park*

It is vitally important that any money you've made from this – whether the guy himself gave you cash, his lawyers paid you off or the newspapers gave you money for a story – is used wisely. How pissed with yourself would you be if, a year down the line, you found it had all gone? What did you spend it on? Did you fritter it away on clothes which are now last season's, a pair of ridiculously expensive shoes on which a heel snapped, or a holiday for all your mates who will never pay you back?

Stop!

Think big, and invest it properly. Either get yourself on the property ladder by laying down a healthy deposit, pay for yourself to go on a degree course that you've always wanted to do, take a career break and go travelling for a year, or set up your own business. Just make it worth your while.*

Making a Positive Out of a Big, Sweaty, Ball-Kicking Negative

When certain things happen after a bad break-up – like seeing him on television or in the newspapers, and being constantly reminded of his presence – it's important to turn any negative emotions that are building up into something positive. This has been by far the best lesson I've learnt from the entire experience.

For me, writing this book has been the ultimate therapy, one of the best things I could have done during my time of heartbreak. I got all of my emotions out onto the page, and it really did make me feel better. Although I'm organised I can also be quite lazy, so whenever I've tried to write books in the past I've always got bored after the first 200 or so words. The momentum would be lost, and I'd end up

---

* Remember also that you must declare all income to the Inland Revenue. You may need an accountant for this. But above all, enjoy it – you've earned it!

watching *Napoleon Dynamite* or trying to teach my dog to shop online instead.

Not this time. My recurring feelings were so strong that it gave me the push I needed to write. And I still have plenty more to say!

During the period of writing this book, I've been called a "self-styled media machine", and even a "well-known football socialite". (I didn't even know they existed, but apparently I am one.) Although I'm not awfully fond of the football socialite thing, something I'm particularly proud of is that a journalist recently heralded me the "saviour of the next generation of WAG wannabe girls". He was commissioned to write a piece about me for a rightwing broadsheet, in which he commended me for being so open about my experiences and laying myself open to criticism in order to educate women on what really happens behind the gated mansions and nightclub doors of the Premiership world. The piece never made it into print – and I know why. Unless I'm portrayed as a ditzy, naïve blonde, they don't want to know.

You may not want to be a writer (it's terribly hard work for not a lot of glory or money!), but whatever you want to do, channel everything you have into it. Let the upset of that skanky footballer who broke your heart light your fire of determination. If you've always wanted to model, but found yourself lost amongst the many hundreds of other wannabes, put your shame to one side and sell the aspect of you dating a footballer. Certain newspapers and lad's mags will love it.

Yes, you'll have to talk about sex, and maybe other things that you don't want to, but just think of Abi Titmuss. She was an educated and articulate woman, yet for about two years all she talked about was sex – but didn't she make an extremely lucrative modelling career out of that?

Maybe you want to be a designer, or a photographer – anything you want to do, use any connections you've made to further yourself. After all, that's what this is all about. Making the best of a bad situation.

DATING AFTER FOOTBALL

*"I wouldn't want my daughter to date a footballer.
I want them to be with a normal guy."* – Suzi Walker,
ex-WAG and a fine example of a WAG don't-wannabe

Sounds easy, doesn't it? Only it's not, believe me. Dating a footballer, then dating an ordinary guy, is like living in a mansion on the Wentworth Estate in Virginia Water before renting a bedsit with rising damp in Basildon. Or perhaps quenching your thirst with Chateldon and then having to overdose on fluoride from the tap.

Footballers are idolised in this country by both men and women alike. More so that our royal family, our rugby or cricket players, or even the genuine heroes who are actually worthy of our admiration. They're just the guys that everyone loves to love ... including any future guys you date.

I remember how, not long after I stopped seeing Wesley, I

decided to try and get back out there and date again. I was out with my friend Kayla in Pangaea and met the hottest, tallest, fittest guy I've ever seen. He was with his equally tall sister, who was called Francesca. "It's a sign!" my drink-fuddled brain was persuaded. He asked me out the very next day and we went to dinner.

A week later I drove to his house in Old Street to watch a movie. We were arguing about something, I can't remember what, and he said that he could prove his point by looking on the internet.

We went into his study, and there it was – the screen saver on the computer was a big, fat picture of WESLEY. *What the … ?*

He must have seen my astonished look, and I thought it was some kind of sick joke, so he just said how much he loved Wesley's team, and that Wesley was "a legend".

Fuck that! That was it for me. How could I date a guy who had a man-crush on the guy I was trying to get over? We didn't see each other again after that.

Other guys have asked me why I'm single and don't want a boyfriend, and I've ended up blurting out the whole sorry tale of how an illicit affair ruined my love life. Some were jealous of the man that they could never live up to; one was too in awe of him, and asked me the weirdest questions. Needless to say, I didn't answer any of them and swiftly deleted him from my phone – and my life.

I've often been on tubes or in bars and overheard men talking about Wesley, and I can't help but crane my neck to listen. Hell, even a guy at my office is obsessed with Wesley's team, and has pre- and post-match analysis phone calls with a friend most days. I can't seem to get away from it.

I thought that maybe it was just because he was a footballer, but I don't think that's the whole problem. I've been on dates with several other footballers since, some of whom are way bigger than Wesley, and if I don't like them then I pretty much just write about them then forget them as fast as I forget what I had for dessert. But the footballing community is a relatively small one and gossip gets around quickly.

One night I went out with a friend to Valmont, a London club, and met a hot guy there. I eventually found out that he was a player in the same team as Wesley. At the time Wesley and I had resumed texting, months after the whole story had come out.

We had fun with the guys in the club, and a couple of us went onto another club in Essex afterwards. And that's all. Honest!

The next day I had furious texts from Wesley, demanding to know what I was doing with his friend, under the apparent belief that he'd stayed at my house and we'd slept together. Nothing could be further from the truth. This guy was SHORT, and I don't do short! Anyway, Wesley refused to believe me and that was the end of that. (A case of the pot calling the kettle black, anyone?)

Other Options

> *"There's no class at Annabelle's anymore. We may*
> *as well have Coleen and Wayne at the next table."*
> – Hugh Warrender, *Tatler*

One good alternative is to date a sophisticated, entrepreneurial man whose interests lie purely in business and the more refined things in life. A boulevardier who vacations at Sandy Lane and Le Quartier Francais in Franschoek, is a regular at Whisky Mist, and has Amy Sacco and Richard Caring on speed dial. He dresses you every week as if you're going to the Crillon Ball and treats you to conversation that is far more interesting than the usual offerings of footballers – which can be uncannily similar to an evening with *Dick and Dom in da Bungalow*.

They tend to think nothing of football, or the guys that play it, and even show disdain for them. There can be no comparisons drawn between the two, they're just too different. When I've been out with footballers they often ask me daft things like, "What is fois gras?", use the wrong cutlery or ask for tomato ketchup. You won't find that with this kind of guy.

Businessmen make far more suitable long-term boyfriends as they're way too busy to go around dogging, roasting and cheating, and are generally far more moral than their ball-kicking counterparts. They also have excellent manners and know exactly where to go. They'll take you to dine at China

Tang, Locanda Locatelli and Cipriani, but will *never* accept seating on the left-hand wall – it's social Siberia. You're far more likely to be rubbing shoulders with Marie-Chantal of Greece rather than Chantelle from *Big Brother* when you're out with one of these guys.

Once you get over your heartbreak and get out there to experience all this world has to offer, you will see that life isn't all about football – but it *is* a good place to start.

CONCLUSION

Well, my friends, we have come to the end. I know, I know – I'm sad too. I've been as open and honest as I can with you, I've revealed things I wouldn't normally admit to myself, let alone to an army of readers. But I hope it's not all been in vain.

I hope we see more girls in Britain aspiring to be so much more than just a WAG. We can't change the cards we're dealt in life, but we can choose how to play the hand. Wesley nearly broke me, but I've come out of this a much stronger person with more ambition than I ever thought possible.

And love? Well, maybe that's too soon, but I can't wait for it to happen one day – once I'm done with my seven-day-week partying schedule!

Girls, please find a man who will love and cherish you for YOU, not for your long hair, big breasts or insatiable appetite for sex. (Although to be fair, those are good selling points!)

Enjoy life while you're young and see and do everything you can. Dance on more tables than a Stringfellows stripper, down more cocktails than the girls in *Sex and the City* and you'll have more tales to tell than J. K. Rowling at the end of it all.

Who knows, maybe you'll see me out and about sometime soon. If you do, come and say hi. I'm the blonde in the corner with the triple vodka, discreetly taking notes. Oh, and if you see me with a footballer of any kind, you have full permission to have a serious word with me!

Until next time …

"Live well. It's the greatest revenge." – The Talmud